MARYLAND
The South's First Casualty

MARYLAND
The South's First Casualty

Bart Rhett Talbert

Rockbridge Publishing Company
Berryville, Virginia

Published by

Rockbridge Publishing Company
P.O. Box 351
Berryville, VA 22611
(703) 955-3980

Photo credits pages 98-127: Alabama Department of Archives and History, 118 bottom; Library of Congress, 100, 114, 124; National Archives, 110; Southern Historical Collection, University of North Carolina, 121, 123; United States Military History Institute, 99 top, 118 top; University of Alabama, 98, 99 bottom, 101,111, 112, 113, 115, 117, 120, 126, 127; Virginia Historical Society, 122, 125.

Library of Congress Cataloging-in-Publication Data

Talbert, Bart Rhett. 1961-
    Maryland: the South's first casualty / Bart Rhett Talbert. — 1st ed.
    p.   cm.
    Includes bibliographical references and index.
    ISBN 1-883522-02-1
    1. Maryland—Politics and government—1861-1865. 2.
Maryland—History—Civil War. 1861-1865. I. Title.
E512.9.T35   1995
975.2'03—dc20   95-17350
                                              CIP

10 9 8 7 6 5 4 3 2 1
FIRST EDITION

For Husky and Captain Buddy

Contents

Foreword

As the series of events of 1860 unfolded in Maryland, the epithet "America in Miniature" was very prevalent. The entire spectrum of political feeling was present, from proponents of slavery to abolitionists. The majority of Free Staters thought they could remain neutral and the state could serve as a buffer zone between the disparate factions until their differences could be resolved.

Maryland was the most important of the border states because of her geographic location. She was, geographically, a southern state. She voted with her sister cotton states in the presidential election of 1860. When it came to secession, geography precluded her from acting until the Commonwealth of Virginia did so, and Virginia was very slow to act.

Bart Talbert does a fine job of describing the political and civilian climate as the forceful suspension of liberties shackled Maryland. His title is very appropriate. The South's first casualty could refer to those Pratt Street civilians who, on April 19, were the first killed in the war; or to the innocents such as Robert W. Davis, who was murdered by cowardly Washington-bound soldiers from their train; or to the citizens of Maryland who were not allowed to decide their own destiny; or to families that were brutally divided, pitting brother against brother, father against son. Indeed, all were the South's first casualties.

This well-researched and well-written account presents the emotions, trials, harrassment and valor of Marylanders during the tragic War Between the States, and draws a clear picture of the steadfast loyalty of her citizens to their Southern neighbors.

Dan Hartzler
New Windsor, Maryland

Acknowledgements

I would like to express my sincere thanks to Dr. Phillip Riley, Dr. John E. Wood, Dr. Steve Guerrier, and especially Dr. Clive Hallman for their patience and hard work. I also express my appreciation to the staffs of the James Madison University history department, library, and graduate school. Though it is difficult to name everyone and every institution that aided me on this project, I express my gratitude for the professionalism and kindness shown me by the staffs of the Hall of Records (Maryland State Archives), the Library of Congress, the National Archives, the Maryland Historical Society, the various county historical and genealogical societies in Maryland, the University of Maryland Library System, the Enoch Pratt Free Library, the Hoole Special Collections at the University of Alabama, and the Maryland Public Library System.

Special thanks I heartily offer Dr. Ray Thompson and Prof. Sylvia Bradley of Salisbury State University for their kindness and guidance; these two are what the profession of history should be all about. For help in the professional presentation and repeated readings of the manuscript I acknowledge the fine efforts of Mr. & Mrs. Gregory Clark, Patricia Fitzgerald Graves, Mr. and Mrs. Detlev Peters, Richard Schraf, Dr. Roger Pearson and friends, Daniel Hartzler, and Laura McCoy Talbert. For the opportunity and respect given by Katherine Tennery and John Hightower I am truly grateful. Without the support and encouragement of my family—Richard, Olive, and Kenneth Talbert—this work would have been impossible. Thanks again. And finally, I thank my father, Robert, for his important help on this project and for introducing me to history so early and so well.

Introduction

When vast amounts of primary source material are available, a people can refer to the facts about their past and decide for themselves what has transpired and how or why they are still affected by these occurrences. But gaining access to the facts is not easy. As many historians have lamented, most people are uninterested in delving deeply into the past because the task seems too difficult for them, and their findings may contradict what they already believe. They may become confused and resent the revelation that they could have been wrong. Yet modern society endures hardships through ignorance and wastes valuable time searching for answers in the hazy light of current ideological or political trends, when a look at the facts under the bright light of a well-documented recent past would make the task of problem solving simple and therefore beneficial to all but a few.

There are literally thousands of examples throughout history of calamities caused by the mass of humanity being unable to provide itself with vision in anything but a hazy light. The history of the United States is full of such examples. It seems that every time United States citizens have gone to war for freedoms they have come out less free than before. As British subjects, North Americans enjoyed more freedoms and paid far fewer taxes than they did as United States citizens once the Constitution began to be manipulated. Northern troops who marched into the South at the beginning of the Civil War certainly did not do so to free the African slaves and reduce the power of their respective Northern states, but that was exactly the outcome. Isolationist America was not chomping at the bit to invade Germany twice in the span of twenty-seven years, but she did, and created or inherited a world empire that is now collapsing upon itself with all the accompanying problems. These examples in American history and the history of any period reveal similar instances of a people fighting and winning wars, yet losing the peace or gaining something that they definitely did not want. This work is intended to deal with misperceptions concerning the Civil War and the state of Maryland, which was caught in the eye of the storm.

Did not our forefathers maintain that the price of freedom is eternal vigilance?

My own earlier readings about my home state planted a subconscious awareness that discrepancies still exist concerning the role and allegiance of this border slave state in the not so distant great national schism. One but has to look at Maryland's state flag, itself a pro-Confederate statement, and hear the state song, a warlike call to southern defense, to guess that the state's history is being reinterpreted incorrectly. When I sampled the post-1960's historical works on Maryland, it became obvious that there was room for further exploration, and upon researching the primary material, I had no doubt that a current restating of the facts was in order.

For instance, in 1964 Charles Lewis Wagandt describes the uprising of April 19, 1861, by Baltimore citizens against what they considered an invasion by Northern troops as "a secessionist mob attack[ing] the soldiers," adds that "many so-called respectable persons joined the town rowdies," then refers to Baltimore as "Mobtown," and finishes with "thus died the first Union soldiers killed by enemy action in the Civil War." That the crowd was composed of respectable citizens acting out of a sense of patriotism has been documented time and again by eyewitnesses and respected historians. Yet Wagandt's assertions are backed up only by a reference to George L. Radcliffe's 1901 work on Governor Thomas H. Hicks. Radcliffe states that the crowd consisted of respectable citizens, who, after the melée, proceeded to hold rallies denouncing the federal invasion and convinced their elected representatives to take any measures deemed necessary to halt any further passage of northern troops over Maryland.

Other modern works—Jean H. Baker's *The Politics of Continuity, Maryland Political Parties From 1858 To 1870*, published in 1973; William J. Evitts' *A Matter of Allegiances, Maryland From 1850 to 1861*, published in 1974; and Richard R. Duncan's chapter on the Civil War in *Maryland, A History 1632-1974*, published in 1974—are equally confused. In successive chapters, these works in essence state that in spite of the actions of the large majority of Maryland's elected representatives—artisans, laborers, militia companies, plantation owners, businessmen, newspaper editors, and farmers in support of the Confederacy and in opposition to the federal government—the state quickly righted itself on the side of the Union. These works are cited repeatedly throughout this book in an attempt to point out their weaknesses and support the truth.

The primary source material from Maryland's Civil War era is meager compared to that of other states, but what exists presents ample evidence and is for the most part readily available for research. The Library of Congress and the National Archives in Washington, D.C., and the Maryland Historical Society and the Peabody Library in Baltimore all house important collections of government documents and public and private correspondence from Maryland's leading men during the war era. The newspapers and periodicals are also an indispensable tool. As the only forms of mass media during this time, they provide important statistics and offer insight into what the people were reading and saying. The bulk of these periodicals can be found in semi-complete form in the Maryland Historical Society, the Enoch Pratt Free Library in Baltimore, and within the holdings of the University of Maryland at its various campuses. The executive papers of Maryland's governors, the documents and journals of the House and Senate, and the debates from the state constitutional conventions can be found in the new Hall of Records in Annapolis.

There is a wealth of secondary source material on Maryland and the Civil War written by eyewitnesses and respected historians unencumbered by the prejudices of the late twentieth century. The most notable are Harold R. Manakee's *Maryland in the Civil War*, 1961; Bradley T. Johnson's *Maryland* in Clement A. Evans', ed., *Confederate Military History*, 1899; Mathew Page Andrews' *History of Maryland: Province And State*, 1929; Thomas J. Scharf's *History of Maryland From the Earliest Period to the Present Day*, 1879; George William Brown's *Baltimore and the Nineteenth of April, 1861*, 1887; Josiah Henry Benton's *Voting in the Field, A Forgotten Chapter Of The Civil War*, 1915; and George L. Radcliffe's *Governor Thomas H. Hicks of Maryland And The Civil War*, 1901. The following works also offer a firsthand insight into the politics and feelings of Marylanders but are of a more military nature: W. W. Goldsborough's *The Maryland Line in the Confederate Army 1861-1865*, 1900; Henry Kyd Douglas' *I Rode With Stonewall*, 1940; and McHenry Howard's *Recollections of a Maryland Confederate Soldier and Staff Officer under Johnston, Jackson and Lee*, 1914.

How many maps depict the North American states arrayed against each other with the North in blue and the South in gray and three or four states in the middle in some greenish hue? The legend identifies the green area as border states, but what does that mean? Textbooks and Civil War anthologies skip over the important issues concerning Missouri, Kentucky, Delaware, and Maryland. Why didn't these states secede from the Union? Would they have seceded if the federal army had respected their sovereignty and rights under the Constitution? Were they northern or southern in sympathy? What was their record of participation in the conflict? How were they affected by Reconstruction? What long-term consequences did the federal victory produce in these states?

This work hopes to shed some light on the answers to these questions as they concern the state of Maryland. One must wonder why an important socio-political and military topic like Maryland's special role in the conflict has not received more attention and clarification.

In researching and composing this work I have experienced a full range of emotions and trials: wandering and searching; learning to express myself; reliving the experiences of others; and frustration over the revelation of human weakness. In the end, I hope I have expressed my case well and perhaps, with all humility, have added something to the world of history that has given me so much.

Chapter One

Maryland Before The War

The dawn of the seventeenth century saw England, Spain, and France vying for dominance of the North American continent. English nobility and gentry were aroused to the great enterprise of colonization and plantation in the New World. As General Bradley T. Johnson, CSA, so aptly put it:

> the spirit that had shattered the Grand Armada and won for commerce the freedom of the seas, was directed to new countries and new States to be founded in North America, where the institutions, the habits, the sentiment and the society of their ancestors were to be transplanted, cultivated and developed, as they had been a thousand years before from the forests of Germany to the shores of Britain.[1]

The King of England chartered companies for the cultivation of the New World and gave large grants of land to individual noblemen and gentlemen of his court. One of these noblemen was Sir George Calvert, a Yorkshire knight of an old family. Calvert, a favorite of King James I, rose rapidly to the post of secretary of state but relinquished this important office after converting to Roman Catholicism in 1625. Calvert, unable to hold public office because of his religion, was raised by the king to the Irish peerage as baron of Baltimore. Lord Baltimore, now the holder of large estates in Ireland, devoted himself to their cultivation and the planning and implementation of his overseas enterprises.[2]

After his failed attempt to establish a colony on Newfoundland, Calvert visited Virginia and, impressed with the climate and improving condition of the planters, petitioned the king for a "precinct of land" in his majesty's dominion on the Chesapeake.[3] George Calvert died before his grant was prepared, but his son and heir, Cecil Calvert, second baron of Baltimore, received the most liberal charter in its terms of any issued up to that time to an English subject.[4] The grant included 13,000 square miles of land and water and the "propriety" was invested with all the powers of the bishop of Durham, who from earliest times had held absolute dominion over his palatinate or dioceses.

Self-government and all the rights of Englishmen were provided for in the charter for all freemen, and the proprietary, as palatine or representative of Lord Baltimore, regulated social laws and behavior. Baltimore had initially established a feudal society based on a landholding aristocracy in Maryland. Ironically, his successful colonization system, which allowed freemen to purchase land cheaply, had worked at cross purposes to his feudal designs. The freemen, disdaining the manorial system of lords and retainers, preferred to work their own small plantations of 250 acres or less. These freemen, who came to control the colonial legislature, challenged Lord Baltimore over the right to frame laws. After each side took turns drawing up charters unacceptable to the other, Calvert decided that such a conflict would adversely affect the financial success of his enterprise and eventually yielded to the colonists. Every man was guaranteed the right of free speech, unless it infringed on the rights of his neighbors, when it was then strictly suppressed. The motto of the Calverts is *Fatti Maschii, Parole Foemine*: deeds are manly, words are womanly, or—as it has always been rendered—Courage and Chivalry.[5] This foundation created a homogeneous and selfless society ready always to help and protect each other in good times and bad. The mindset and spirit in Maryland for generations had been "one for all, and all for one."[6]

This magnanimous aspect of Maryland's character exhibited itself strongly in 1774 when, in solidarity with the people of Massachusetts, the colonists held their own tea party by burning the *Peggy Stewart* in Annapolis Harbor on October 19. The following year, upon hearing that Bostonians were killed by British regulars, the men of Maryland quickly formed into companies and battalions for defense and along with the women and children formed an association boycotting imported goods as long as Boston Harbor remained closed to trade. Following the battle of Breed's Hill, popularly known as Bunker Hill, Maryland sent two companies five hundred fifty miles from Frederick to Boston in support of the New Englanders. All this was done for a cause that did not affect the citizens directly, for Maryland enjoyed a just and liberal system led by governor Robert Eden, one of the most popular men in the province.

Except for the short campaign from Elk to Brandywine in September of 1777, no British troops ever occupied Maryland soil, but the state remained true to its colonial neighbors. Maryland's citizen soldiers fought fiercely on battlefields outside the colony and gained a reputation for dependability unsurpassed during the War of Independence.[7] Marylanders stood and died with Stirling at Long Island to save the Continental Army; charged at Eutaw to check the victorious British from routing Greene; drove the British line at Cowpens; and with their bayonets broke the solid front of the Grenadier Guards at Guilford.[8] In 1860, as in the time of the Revolution, the people of Maryland were patriots and did not wish to see the Union which they had always supported and fought for torn asunder. But the coming political and possibly military struggle between the two ways of life in America would certainly directly involve them. How they would control their own destiny was foremost in the thoughts of their leaders.

During the twenty years prior to 1860, Maryland's economic scope and strength had advanced. Most of this growth had been toward the north and west, drawn by the growing network of canals and railroads. Most of the inner growth was in the form of Irish and German immigrants moving into Maryland from the Northern states. But under the surface, what were the feelings and thrust of the Maryland conscience? To answer this question one must look to and beyond the foundation of the state to its development and sectional allegiances.

One responsibility of the New World was to provide raw materials for the mother country, and it was referred to simply as the Plantations. There were, originally, two great centers of English colonization on the North American continent—those of New England and the Chesapeake settlements of Maryland and Virginia. The latter, because of its fertile coastal plain and broad rivers extending far inland, was ideally suited for cultivating and exporting cash crops. The early inhabitants of Maryland and Virginia fought over boundaries and religious issues; but this conflict was more an extension of disagreements in England than a real contest between two ways of life and eventually the two colonies formed the greatest of bonds.

It was this Chesapeake source of Maryland and Virginia, along with a consequential and similar development in the Carolinas, from which the rest of the South was populated and received its cultural stamp. The Carolina land grants were made by Charles II to his favorites as reward for their loyalty during the English civil war and in an effort to create profitable plantations like those of the Chesapeake. Many of the men who pioneered and created the states that eventually became part of the Confederacy, such as Sam Houston and others not so famous, were at one time from the tidewater states. It was the Kentucky rifles and the woodsmen of the Carolinas, for the most part transplanted Marylanders and Virginians, who took and held the wilderness from the savages and their French and Spanish allies. The first Americans in Louisiana were called Kaintucks by the locals because they were frontiersmen from Kentucky and Virginia. This great western movement had its roots in the Tidewater and once the land had been conquered was given over unselfishly to the Union for the good of all United States citizens.[9]

Scotch-Irish and German immigrants, along with the original Tidewater settlers, poured through the Cumberland gap or the Carolinas on their way west. They came to the New World not only for religious and political freedoms but also for land and fortune, and thus they were drawn to the lush forests and fertile soil of the lower South.

Small farmers and large plantation owners inundated the South, imitating the life of the Tidewater planter or his ancestor on the English countryside. This westward movement and the subsequent establishment of states was an eighteenth and early nineteenth century phenomenon. Maryland was a Southern state for almost two hundred years before the Cotton-Belt saw colonization and statehood. Most of the deep South was under the Union flag for only about forty years before the outbreak of the Civil War.

Highlighting this forgotten reality are the facts that at war's outbreak nearly fifty percent of the white population of New Orleans had been born outside of the United States and that well over half of the remainder had been born outside the state. Only one in fourteen exercised his right to vote in New Orleans during the presidential election of 1860, compared with Maryland, where one of every six citizens voted.

The southern slave states, led by Virginia and her great statesmen, dominated American politics following independence from England. Historian James McPherson writes:

> The selection of Supreme Court justices by geographical circuits gave the slave states, with their larger territory, a majority on the Supreme Court. And the South's domination of the Democratic party allowed the section to wield political power out of proportion to its population. For two-thirds of the years from 1789 to 1861, the presidents of the United States, the speakers of the House and presidents *pro tem* of the Senate, and

the chairmen of key congressional committees were Southerners.[10]

But by the gradual abolition of slavery north of the Chesapeake, where the institution was economically unfeasible, obsolete or socially burdensome, the Northern or free states began to dominate the national government through sheer numbers. McPherson continues:

> Before 1850, Congress admitted free and slave states alternately to the Union, enabling the South to maintain parity in the Senate (at fifteen slave states and fifteen free states by 1848) even though the region's slower population growth reduced the South to a permanent minority in the House and in the electoral college.

But:

> By 1860, the free states had a population of nineteen million, and the slave states just over twelve million. Four million of the latter were slaves. The election of a president by a Northern antislavery party in 1860 was the handwriting on the wall. To escape the perceived threat to their way of life, most of the slave states seceded.

The South wished to safeguard its regional interests under the Constitution while the North was anxious to bring its numerical preponderance to bear in dominating the nation without interference in government from what they held to be the inordinate power of the slave states.[12]

The North, with its commercial and expansionist aspirations thus threatened, began to agitate the slavery issue for, as it was framed by the press and prominent abolitionists, religious and moral reasons. Realistically, however, the reasons were overwhelmingly political, and the actions taken were no more than a thinly veiled attempt to stem any resurgence or spread of Southern power. In 1856, a leading abolitionist newspaper complained that the large majority of self-styled abolitionists were merely self-serving businessmen and politicians whose "main impulse is to secure the new Territories for Free White Labor, with little or no regard for the interests of negroes, free or slave."[13] This struggle took many forms, but two of the earliest and most conspicuous were the Missouri Compromise and South Carolina's nullification of the tariff law of 1832.

In the first instance, Missouri, a territory advocating the institution of slavery, was denied statehood by Northern votes in the United States

House of Representatives, because the admission of that territory to the Union would destroy the balance of power in the senate. Missouri was held out of the Union until Maine, a free territory, was readied for statehood, and the two were entered together in 1821, as a compromise, and equilibrium was maintained. The second major confrontation occurred in 1831, as South Carolina nullified a tariff law that protected Northern manufacturers and taxed the rest of the country for their benefit. The South Carolinians, acting on the theory presented by Thomas Jefferson's Kentucky resolutions of 1798 and 1799 and expanded by John C. Calhoun, held that the government created by the compact of the states was not made the exclusive or final judge of the extent of the powers delegated to itself.[14] The secession of South Carolina and possible civil war were averted only when the federal government reached a compromise solution and passed a new tariff bill in 1833.[15]

So the struggle continued, sometimes smoldering under the surface or at other times erupting onto the national scene. These eruptions were bitter contests concerning slavery in land acquired from the Louisiana Purchase and the war with Mexico, as well as the struggle over the tariff issue. The problems were exacerbated by Northern agitation aimed at diminishing the power of the slave states and were only quelled by last ditch compromises that merely served to forestall the inevitable conflagration.

In the latter part of the twentieth century, the mass of Americans have accepted the notion that the Civil War was fought solely to free the Negro slaves, when in reality the causes of the war were many, some dating from the ratification of the Constitution. It was the abolitionists who fanned the slavery issue into one of national importance. Few Americans agreed with the abolitionist wing of the Republican party on the issue of slavery and, as they pressed their designs against the South, the arguments became heated, with hatred often overcoming reason.[16]

Slavery had existed in Maryland from colonial times. The buying and selling of slaves was a thriving business, and some dealers went to the excess of kidnapping free Negroes and selling them into captivity. Various attempts were made by the government of Maryland to discourage the kidnappings and also to restrict the slave trade. During the eighteenth century, higher and higher taxes were levied on the importation of slaves and the general assembly finally prohibited the trans-Atlantic trade after 1783.

Manumission, especially upon the death of the owner, became popular at the beginning of the nineteenth century. In an older state, such as

Maryland, many slave and owner families had been together for generations. Slaveowners who were nearing the end of their lives or relinquishing their agricultural holdings were loath to sell slaves off to an uncertain future and often freed them. Of the 111,079 Negroes in Maryland in 1790, 8,043 were free and 103,036 were slaves, a ratio of roughly 14 slaves for every one free Negro. In contrast, by 1860 the numbers had become almost equal; of 171,131 Negroes in Maryland, 87,189 were slaves and 83,942 were free. The majority of the free Negroes lived in the central and western regions of the state.[17]

In spite of this trend toward manumission, Marylanders began to experience problems with Northern resistance to the Fugitive Slave Law, established at the signing of the Constitution (Article IV, Section 2), which provided for the recovery of runaways and was reaffirmed in the Compromise of 1850. Slaveholders or their agents were allowed to pursue runaways into free territories or states, and upon proof of ownership they could request assistance from local authorities in the recovery of the fugitives. Problems arose when slaves would flee to the neighboring free state of Pennsylvania, where citizens would help them evade capture, sometimes even resorting to violence against the slave's lawful owners. There were two cases in particular that were the source of much contention in Maryland.

In June of 1847, James H. Kennedy of Hagerstown, Washington County, went north to Carlisle, Pennsylvania, for the purpose of claiming fugitive slaves. After presenting proof of ownership, he was attacked outside of the courthouse by an abolitionist mob and so brutally beaten that he died soon thereafter. Four years later, in 1851, Edward Gorsuch of Baltimore County, accompanied by his son, several friends and a deputy United States marshal, pursued fugitive slaves into Lancaster County, Pennsylvania. Not long after they arrived in the town of Christiana, the group was attacked by an abolitionist mob. Gorsuch was murdered, and his son was severely injured. These attacks and similar incidents contributed to the feelings of anger and hatred in Maryland toward abolitionists in particular and Northerners in general.[18]

One of the basic themes in Maryland politics before, during, and after the war was what to do about the increase in the "hate[d] free Negro population."[19] The best known and most effective organization dealing with the problem of freed slaves was the Colonization Society of Maryland, founded in 1831, for the purpose of encouraging the return of free Negroes to Africa.[20] The society received support from private contributions, and the Maryland government appropriated $10,000 annually for twenty-six

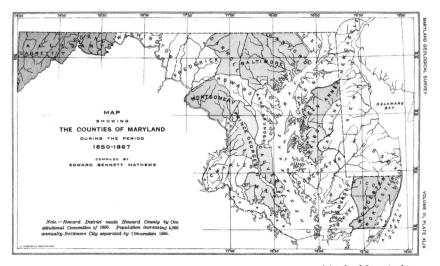

Maryland State Archives

Maryland counties 1850-1867.

years to promote the project.[21] The undertaking was quite a success, with the establishment of a viable colony on Africa's west coast, known as the state of Maryland in the nation of Liberia. A region known as Maryland exists to this day in Liberia.

The tariff and slavery issues, however, were not the major problems between North and South. The decades-long struggle and subsequent war was fought over which would ultimately hold sovereignty—the states or the national government. The southern states were concerned about who would ultimately control the way of life in their region—the international, capitalistic, urban North or the aristocratic, nationalistic, agrarian South. Moreover, they wondered who would print and control the money, and whether minority rights (by the 1860s the rights of Southerners), a definite concern of the founding fathers, would be respected under the Constitution.

Southern sympathy was strong throughout Maryland, but it was almost universal in the six southern counties and the Eastern Shore. Few immigrants had settled in these areas, which were dominated by large plantations producing cash crops. The residents of southern Maryland and the Eastern Shore retained their British background and attempted to emulate the lifestyle of the English countryside. Like the rest of the agricultural South, these regions wanted to see low tariffs, thereby facilitating the purchase of less expensive European goods instead of the artificially inflated products from Northern manufacturers.[22]

Politically, these southern regions had changed little from colonial days. The zeal of their leading men for public service earned these citizens respect and power throughout the state. For generations they had solved their problems through county and state governments, and, therefore, were naturally strong believers in the concept of states rights. Like the rest of the South, they believed that the individual states were more powerful than the federal government.[23] Since the states had entered the Union and made concessions of their own will, they could, therefore, elect to leave it when the system of government became oppressive.[24]

Maryland, however, like most states, had regional differences; hers can be ascribed to two main facts. One, the diverse geography enjoyed by the state insured that there would be economically unique and separate styles of life. And two, the central and western counties of the state, lying on the border with the North, naturally developed commercial ties with that section of the country that attracted German and Irish immigrants who had altogether different values and motives from the earlier English settlers.[25]

Central and western Maryland had experienced appreciable change since the days of the colonies. Of the 590,000 Marylanders in 1860, one in five was born in another country or state, usually a Northern one. Many of the immigrants were tradesmen or worked their small farms in the rocky country of central and western Maryland. Most came from Europe, where they had little or no say in their government. After settling in Maryland, they were eager to become citizens in order to participate in the political process.

Agriculture, the leading industry in this section of Maryland, was conducted on small farms that produced grain, livestock, fruit, vegetables and dairy products. In most cases a man and his son, sometimes with the help of a few laborers, got the job done. Slavery, therefore, was not prevalent in the central and western regions.

Manufacturing, steadily growing in upper Maryland with factories in Baltimore City, Baltimore, Harford, Frederick, Washington and Carroll counties, had little use for slaves. They needed skilled or semi-skilled workers who had the expertise to operate modern machinery. Also, unlike their southern neighbors, most people associated with manufacturing were in favor of high tariffs to inflate the price of their products and protect them from European competition.[26]

While transportation improved throughout central and western Maryland, the other parts of the state remained relatively isolated. Projects like the National Road, the three canals, and the railroads created business and social ties with states to the north and west.[27] Because the federal government participated in these projects, the people of these regions had no reason to fear its quest for power. A small number of Marylanders who directly benefitted from these projects and newly arriving immigrants believed that the federal government had rights over the states on a limited basis.

Supporting higher tariffs and vying with the agriculturists from southern Maryland for political power within the state was one thing, but the belief that the federal government had the right to hold the southern states in the Union by force was quite another issue, one that was vigorously denied by the vast majority of Marylanders.[28] Also by the late 1850s, the large number of free Negroes in Maryland were competing with the newly arrived Irish and German immigrants for the coveted semi-skilled positions in the manufacturing industry, a competition that at times elicited a bloody response from immigrants. These immigrants were soon to find themselves on the horns of a dilemma: they wanted to support a strong federal government, but it was soon to be run by a party that would coerce the southern states and press for abolition as a war aim.[29] As we shall see, any pro-federal, not to be misconstrued as pro-Union, feelings that may have existed in central and western Maryland prior to the summer of 1860 changed radically when the Northern army of occupation began the iron rule of martial law the following spring.

The issues of tariff, slavery in the territories, and states rights, including the right of secession, were as old as the nation. They loomed large on the political horizon as the election of 1860 approached, and once again they played an important role in an American presidential election. The industrial North and the agricultural South could only find disagreement, which was fast degenerating into bitterness, as the election approached.[30]

Those who attempt to convince us that the sole cause of the war was slavery, or that the Northern troops marched south to free the African slave must remember two things. One, only a few people in the North, the extreme radical abolitionists, wanted to end slavery altogether. The newspapers, diaries and letters of the day tell us that the overwhelming majority of Northerners—citizens, officers and men in the ranks—resented the fact that the war had taken on an abolitionist flavor due to Lincoln's political maneuverings. And two, those Northerners who were concerned about slavery simply did not want Southerners bringing their slaves into the territories; they were not abolitionists. In fact, they did not want blacks of any kind in the territories.

The circumstances and history of political parties in Maryland are as varied and complex as her demographic and geographic features. In the decade prior to the election of 1860, Maryland was controlled by the Know-Nothing or American Party.[31] The Know-Nothings, originally a Northern movement, were a product of political nativism, a reaction by American citizens threatened by the combination of immigration, political disaffection, sectional stress, and by a sense of lost goals and values.[32] This movement, little known because of its origins in secret societies, burst onto the political scene in the early 1850s and received national support but was particularly strong in the border states.

Marylanders went through a stage of political disillusionment in the early 1850s as a result of changes in electoral behavior and morality. They were repulsed by the vulgarity of contemporary politics and the type of individual who engaged in it.[33] Election violence, especially in Baltimore City, became common-place as weapon-wielding mobs sought to prevent opposition voters from reaching the polls. Political allegiances shifted during this period of tight, one-party control of election wards and districts. Baltimore, which was Democratic in the 1840s, became the political barony of the Know-Nothings, and the Democrats began to carry what once was Whig-dominated southern Maryland. This lack of form and dignity in the political process produced voter apathy to the point that in an age when turnout had been almost universal in Maryland, only seven out of ten of the eligible citizens bothered to exercise this hard won right.[34]

By the late 1850s, the Democrats, in an attempt to wrest control of Maryland from the Know-Nothings, began to ignore divisive local matters and concentrate on solidifying the party by addressing national issues. Local papers were filled with articles about the Dred Scott decision (1857) and President James Buchanan's policy toward Kansas instead of the usual debates concerning only Maryland. The Democrats spoke about Liberty, Constitution, and Union in a way that meant defense of the South and pulled many former Know-Nothings across party lines. An article in the Baltimore *Sun*, August 26, 1859, quotes a former American party congressman, Augustus R. Sollers:

> I am forced into the ranks of the Democratic party, despite prejudices engendered by twenty years of active opposition, because I behold in that party the only bulwark of Southern rights, the only political organization capable of stemming the tide of Northern fanaticism and of supporting in their integrity the Constitution and Union.[35]

Conservative Know-Nothings tried to straddle the slavery debate and concentrate on state issues, but as the decade came to a close and members bolted to the Democrats, those who were left could not help being labelled as siding with the Republicans. To Maryland Democrats, the Republican party was an anti-southern movement led by its radical core of abolitionist extremists. This association with the Black Republicans dampened any hopes the Know-Nothing Party, as it had formerly existed, held of maintaining a wide following in Maryland, because almost no one wanted to see any increase in the free Negro population.[37]

Maryland's efforts to colonize freed Negroes in Africa had, indeed, experienced some success, but the numbers were against the enterprise. One of every five inhabitants of the state was a black, and the decade of the 1840s saw a twenty percent increase in the free Negro population, with nothing to indicate a change for the 1850s.[38] Many Marylanders began to conclude that blacks should choose between going into slavery or leaving the state.[39] Maryland slaveholders even went so far as to consider the possibility of expelling all free Negroes. This was proposed and debated during an 1859 convention of slaveholders chaired by Democratic senator James Pearce. Realizing that such a law would affect a considerable number of the state's household and agricultural laborers, the convention declined to recommend to the state legislature that Maryland become a haven for white men.[40]

If changes wrought by immigration and economic expansion in the twenty years prior to the war were dividing the state, this was brought to an abrupt halt by the results of and events immediately preceding the election of 1860. In July of 1859, an event took place in Maryland and in neighboring Virginia which left no doubt in the minds of yet undecided citizens as to the reality of Northern hostility toward the South and slavery. John Brown, the notorious abolitionist from Kansas, already wanted for the murder of several people, descended on Maryland intent on furthering his nefarious designs. Accompanied by his sons and followers, Brown began clandestine operations. From his rented headquarters at the Kennedy farm several miles southwest of Frederick, Maryland, he planned to seize the federal arsenal at Harpers Ferry and with the captured arms touch off a slave insurrection. Brown then planned to move southward through Appalachia, freeing slaves as he went. Using the mountain chain as his impregnable fortress, he hoped to strike deep into the South and form a large sovereign state composed of freed slaves. Eventually he hoped to bring an end to the institution of slavery in the United States forever.[41]

The arsenal at Harpers Ferry was located in a remote and sleepy area of what was then Virginia. Brown's group surprised the peacetime garrison late on Sunday, October 16, and enjoyed some initial success. As one newspaper reported, there "silently and stealthily descended upon Harpers Ferry under cover of darkness upon a Sabbath evening an armed band of murderous insurgents for the purpose of exciting a servile and bloody insurrection."[42]

Upon learning of the raid, public reaction was swift and violent. Militia companies from Maryland and Virginia, some coming from as far as Baltimore, converged on the arsenal. Of the Maryland militia companies, only one, that from Prince Georges County, was not from the central or western region. Brown's party, now holding a few hostages and a number of Negroes brought in from the surrounding area by force,[43] was penned up in a railroad engine house. There was no bargaining with known murderers by the officer in command.

On Tuesday, October 18, Colonel Robert E. Lee, U.S. Army, accompanied by future Confederate general J.E.B. Stuart, led a group of U.S. Marines and stormed the arsenal. Ten of Brown's men were killed or mortally wounded in the ensuing fray, and he and the survivors were captured and charged with eight counts of murder, treason against Virginia, and conspiring with slaves to rebel.

Maryland newspapers carried front-page headlines of the raid, the capture and subsequent trial of the conspirators, and the execution of John Brown by the commonwealth of Virginia. Brown's enterprise was a complete fiasco—instead of sparking an insurrection, it had the opposite effect of awakening and hardening the resolution of Marylanders to resist abolitionist attacks on their society and state.[44]

Afterward, when the futile nature of the raid became known, the event "dwindle[d] into insignificance." But Brown's adventure brought to mind the horrors of bloody, servile insurrections such as had occurred in Southampton County, Virginia, Jamaica, Haiti and Santa Domingo. Marylanders were indignant and bitter when they learned that Brown received aid for his undertaking from six New England abolitionists. North-South relations were further strained when from pulpits and in the press some in the North proclaimed Brown a hero and martyr.[45] There was an ambient feeling that there could be no compromise, and that violence must follow if the North continued to promote such attacks as this on a great national agreement that had made the Union possible.

Not wishing to exacerbate sectional problems to the detriment of their party's chances in the upcoming election, prominent Republicans such as

University of Alabama

Thomas Hicks, governor of Maryland
1857-1861

Abraham Lincoln and William H. Seward disavowed the actions of Brown. But the people of Maryland, the District of Columbia, and Virginia were unconvinced and blamed the Republicans for the current level of fanaticism and hatred. A citizen of the capital was quoted as saying that "a heavy responsibility falls upon persons in the North as abettors of Murder and Treason."[46] The militia companies that participated in quelling the insurrection were hailed as heroes and the victory against "Northern fanaticism" was celebrated in grand parades.[47] Marylanders became suspicious of outsiders who might repeat actions similar to those of Brown. Strangers were expected to have a good reason for their presence and make known their future intentions.[48] This mood also heightened an awareness of what a Republican victory in the presidential election of 1860 would mean, and consequently, the Maryland legislature responded in 1860 by appropriating $70,000 to arm the militia.[49]

The Democratic party, already on the rise in Maryland, benefitted tremendously from John Brown's raid. As the champions of Southern rights, the Democrats were able to saddle the Know-Nothings with the blame for the incident at Harpers Ferry.[50] The weakness of Maryland's governor Thomas Hicks, a Know-Nothing, and the pro-Republican tendencies of the new American party became decisive issues in the statewide elections of 1859. The American party in turn tried to wrest the initiative from their opponents by accusing the Democrats of political badgering on "Harpers Ferry ... [and] the Niggers." This tactic was viewed only as an attempt to cloud the real issues and unfairly influence voters.[51]

The voters agreed with the Democrats concerning the "ineffectiveness" of Governor Hicks and "the feeble Know-Nothing allegiance to protect the South," by sweeping the party into offices both county and statewide.[52] Unable to shed the blame for Harpers Ferry, and sensing doom for their political careers and party, disgruntled members of the

American party identified the incident as the turning point in the election and bitterly called the new state assembly of 1859, the "John Brown Legislature."[53]

Fresh from their victories in November of 1859, the Democrats in Maryland began a statewide reform movement. Disgusted by corrupt elections and the accompanying violence, they instituted new judicial and election procedures across Maryland, but especially in the city of Baltimore, where control of the police force was taken over by state authorities. The Know-Nothing party of Baltimore, by attempting to stem the Democratic surge in 1859 with their favorite tactic of street violence, had finally gone too far. The resulting confrontations were the bloodiest ever in a city infamous for electoral rowdyism. The Know-Nothings' attempt to ensure the outcome one last time by violence guaranteed that they would never win another election.

The Democrats, now in control of the legislature and prompted by various petitions calling for a reduction in the number of free Negroes, began to legislate on this issue through their control of the Committee on Colored Population.[54] Chairman Curtis M. Jacobs summed up the feelings of many when he said "free [negroism] is an excrescence, a blight, a mildew, a fungus, hanging on to and corrupting the social and moral elements of our people."[55] A set of laws, subject to county approval, were passed in 1860: manumissions were prohibited, colonizations and departures of Negroes from the state were encouraged, free Negroes were entitled to renounce their freedom and choose their own masters, and free Negroes, now required to be registered by county commissioners, could be sold into slavery for minor criminal offenses.[56]

The Know-Nothing delegates were split and all but one Democrat voted for this legislation, aimed not at strengthening the institution of slavery but at controlling the free Negro population. The success of these bills endeared racially conscious Marylanders and slaveholders to the Democrats. As a matter of course, the opposition press accused the rising Democrats of "Nigger Agitation,"[57] but it must be remembered that half of the Know-Nothing or American party delegates voted for this legislation as well. The Democrats in turn made no attempts to deny their interest in the "colored question."[58]

The Democratic national convention met in Charleston, South Carolina, on April 11, 1860, with full delegations present from every state in the Union. The Democrats were in harmony on all issues except the doctrine of non-intervention by Congress with slavery in the territories. A rift developed when, in a close majority vote, the right of territorial

The Presidential Election of 1860 in Maryland
Votes Cast for Each Candidate, with Percentage

County	Breckinridge	Bell	Douglas	Lincoln
Allegany	979 (23.2)	1521 (36.0)	1203 (28.5)	522 (12.3)
Anne Arndl	1107 (47.1)	1041 (48.4)	98 (4.5)	3 (0.0)
Baltimore	3305 (46.0)	3388 (47.2)	449 (6.3)	37 (0.5)
Calvert	386 (46.6)	399 (48.1)	43 (5.3)	1 (0.0)
Caroline	616 (42.8)	712 (49.4)	100 (6.9)	12 (0.9)
Carroll	1791 (39.9)	2295 (51.2)	339 (7.6)	59 (1.3)
Cecil	1506 (39.1)	1792 (46.6)	393 (10.2)	158 (4.1)
Charles	723 (60.4)	430 (35.9)	38 (3.2)	6 (0.5)
Dorchester	1176 (46.9)	1265 (50.5)	31 (1.2)	35 (1.4)
Frederick	3167 (43.2)	3616 (49.3)	445 (6.1)	103 (1.4)
Harford	1527 (43.0)	1862 (52.4)	82 (2.3)	81 (2.3)
Howard	530 (34.2)	830 (53.5)	189 (12.3)	1 (0.0)
Kent	694 (41.8)	852 (51.3)	74 (4.5)	42 (2.4)
Montgomery	1125 (46.3)	1155 (47.6)	99 (4.1)	50 (2.0)
Pr.Georges	1048 (53.0)	885 (44.8)	43 (2.2)	1 (0.0)
Qn. Anne's	879 (46.9)	908 (48.5)	87 (4.6)	0 (0.0)
St. Mary's	920 (67.1)	261 (19.0)	190 (13.9)	1 (0.0)
Somerset	1339 (45.2)	1536 (51.8)	89 (3.0)	2 (0.0)
Talbot	898 (50.1)	793 (44.3)	98 (5.6)	2 (0.0)
Washington	2475 (45.7)	2567 (47.4)	283 (5.2)	95 (0.7)
Worcester	1425 (55.6)	1048 (40.9)	90 (3.5)	0 (0.0)
County Totals	27326 (44.0)	29156 (46.9)	4463 (7.2)	1211 (1.9)
Baltimore City	14956 (49.1)	12604 (41.5)	1503 (5.0)	1083 (4.5)
Maryland	42282 (45.8)	41760 (45.2)	5966 (6.5)	2294 (2.5)

legislatures to pass laws against slave property was affirmed. This victory of the faction led by Stephen A. Douglas over President Buchanan's position broke up the convention, which later reconvened in Baltimore. The divisive mood persisted. The eight Maryland delegates, along with those from the other Southern states, again walked out, this time to hold their own convention and nominate John C. Breckinridge of Kentucky. The remaining delegates, calling themselves the National Democrats, chose Douglas as their presidential nominee.

National Archives
Bradley T. Johnson

The National Democratic party, or the Douglas faction—not to be confused with the Democratic National party of Breckinridge—was at a decided disadvantage in Maryland from the beginning, for two reasons. First and foremost, Marylanders clearly joined Douglas and Republican nominee Lincoln together as unacceptably anti-Southern. Second, the Breckinridge Democrats, led by Bradley T. Johnson, "the handsome, goateed Frederick county newspaper editor and future Confederate general,"[59] controlled the party machine in Maryland. Johnson also enjoyed the support of many dedicated and influential politicians and newspaper editors so important to successful campaigning. Breckinridge was able to blast Douglas for his evasion of the slavery issue. When Douglas responded with his doctrine of "popular sovereignty" as a remedy for the slavery issue in the territories, Breckinridge successfully labelled this stance as unconstitutional, dangerous, and therefore totally unacceptable to the South.[60]

The Breckinridge Democrats also carried their campaign fight to the Republicans and the new Constitutional Unionist party. They reasoned that even if the election of Lincoln was unavoidable, a large vote for Breckinridge would proclaim that Maryland rebuked Republican "radical and inflammatory theories." Furthermore, no "overt act" would be made by the new administration if it were made clear that agitation over the slavery issue had gone far enough.[61] The Constitutional Unionists were criticized for evading the issue of slavery in the territories,[62] as well as for their lack of a stated and serious campaign platform. Breckinridge made light of this last occurrence when he said:

> Gentlemen, they tell us that they are advocating the principles of "the Constitution, the Union, and the enforcement of the laws." I presume that there is scarcely a man in this assembly—perhaps no one North or South—who will admit that he is against the constitution, the Union, and enforcement of the laws.[63]

The Constitutional Union party in Maryland comprised the remnants of the old Whig and Know-Nothing organizations. John Pendleton Kennedy, head of the organization in Maryland, worked hard to channel Know-Nothing support into the new national party.[64] This combination was strong numerically and enjoyed the support of a considerable press.[65] This was a party based on anti-sectional attitudes, which attempted to fill the ideological gap between Breckinridge and Douglas. The Constitutional Unionists considered the slavery question already settled by geography and climate and saw silence as the best way to deal with it. They chose the rather bland former Whig John Bell of Tennessee to run for president on their non-committal platform that called for support of the "Constitution, Union and Enforcement of the Laws."[66]

University of Alabama

Henry Winter Davis

Such a combination could not be without various shades of opinion, and the Constitutional Unionists fluctuated appreciably on a number of issues. The conservative faction of Bell's party supported the economic policies of the old Whigs, was friendly to the South and slavery, and detested the Republicans and the faction in their own party led by a U.S. congressman from Maryland, Henry Winter Davis.[67] The American or Know-Nothing faction held sectionalism to be dangerous, believed the territorial slavery question was insignificant, and strongly advocated a protective tariff.[68]

It is understandable then that these factions within the Constitutional Unionist framework had a tenuous allegiance at best. The feelings for Lincoln ranged from abhorrence by the conservatives to the belief by the moderates that he would be amiable to the South if elected and could be worked with in time. Yet the voice of this moderate group, the Baltimore *Daily Clipper*, also came out strongly for the South and slavery. The paper opposed secession while reporting that

USMHI

Montgomery Blair

"thirty thousand native born voters uphold slavery." Bell men courted Baltimore voters by arguing that their interests would be best served by maintaining the Union and continuing their business ties with the large slaveholders and monied interests in the South, whom they believed to be Unionists.[69]

The goal of the Constitutional Unionists was a tricky one. To win, they must convince Marylanders that they were pro-slavery, anti-Republican and pro-tariff, and hope to get away with evading the territorial slavery issue, while playing down any connection to the old Know-Nothing movement and resisting any inferences of cooperation with the hated Black Republican party.

The only real chance the Republicans had of even playing a small part during the election of 1860 in Maryland was to ally themselves with the Constitutional Unionists. This opportunity was lost when the Republicans nominated Lincoln in Chicago on May 18, 1860. A Unionist newspaper summed it up in this way: "It is folly to organize the Republican Party, it will only get a thousand votes in the State."[70] In fact, it was dangerous to declare oneself a Republican supporter in Maryland. The first Republican nominating convention held in the state, in April of 1860, was broken up by a protesting mob and had to adjourn to a private residence, where Montgomery Blair was chosen to preside.[71]

Blair, who worked hard to rid the party of its abolitionist stigma in

Maryland, stated the two great measures for which the Republicans stood: a homestead law, which would prevent the Africanization of the territories, and the colonization of free Negroes on what he termed "Jefferson's Plan," in an undetermined area near the United States.[72] He made it clear that his party did not favor equality of the races or amalgamation, did not wish to touch slavery where it already existed, and was first and foremost a white man's party.[73]

The Republicans felt impelled to issue a circular some months before the election in an attempt to clarify their position on the great question of the campaign: Shall slavery be nationalized and extended, or shall it be limited? The belief that the Republicans wished to abolish slavery by force, and to elevate the Negro to a social equality with the whites, was denounced as ignorant and malicious. The circular re-emphasized that the Republicans were a white man's party which strove to protect and "ennoble" free labor.[74] Blair later added that "any law of the Federal government abolishing slavery in Maryland would be as void and nugatory as an act of the British Parliament."[75]

Try as they would to concentrate on other issues, such as the need for a tariff to develop industry and bring revenues, or the need to stop election violence and clean up the rotten borough system, the Republicans could not shake their emancipationist label. As election day drew near, the Wide Awakes, notorious Lincoln activists from the North, held a parade in Baltimore during which they were pelted with stones and rotten eggs. The Reverend French S. Evans, editor of the Baltimore *Patriot*, spoke with difficulty amidst hissing, laughter, shouts, nose-blowing, and the hurling of rotten eggs. He continued: "What, I ask, is the Republican party? A voice—'Niggers'—and great laughter." The feelings were intensely bitter and the Republicans were shielded from serious injury only by police intervention.[76] A similar incident occurred at Baltimore's Richmond market, where a speaker posed the question: "Who is the Republican party?" The crowd answered in unison: "The Niggers."[77]

The little support that the Republicans did receive in Maryland came from the German communities, and yet this was sharply divided between the old stock, who had immigrated in the 18th century, and the new wave from the 1840s and 1850s who favored abolition. Normally the vanguard of Republican support, the German communities in Maryland showed little enthusiasm for Lincoln. The future president was rejected in Baltimore wards that were predominantly German, receiving less than three percent of the vote.[78] One of the two main German language newspapers, *Der Deutsche Correspondent*, even came out in support of

Breckinridge.[79]

John C. Breckinridge, a National Democrat whose platform endorsed the Dred Scott decision, protested Northern agitation against "the institutions of the slave States" and upheld the Fugitive Slave Act, won the election with almost forty-six percent of Maryland's poll, defeating Bell by fewer than a thousand votes and thereby receiving the state's eight electoral votes. Breckinridge received support from all over the state, but was strongest in areas of black and slaveholding populations. The nominee of the Northern Democrats, Stephen A. Douglas, fared poorly in Maryland, receiving only six percent of the popular vote, but combined with Breckinridge tallied a majority for the Democrats. These victories signalled the resurgence of the party in the state.

John Bell was a large slaveholder and former Jackson Democrat turned Whig, whose vigorous defense of the Union had won him the nomination for president on the Constitutional Union ticket in 1860. Bell's numbers in Maryland, over forty-five percent of the popular vote, mirrored his successes in areas of former Know-Nothing strength. He carried only Virginia, Kentucky, and Tennessee, essentially all border slave states. Bell, who had opposed secession and insisted Lincoln's policy toward the South would be moderate, like most Constitutional Unionists changed his opinion drastically following the new administration's call for troops to coerce the slave states. Afterward, Bell openly advocated Southern resistance and classified himself as a rebel. He spent the war years in Georgia and returned to Tennessee in 1865.[81]

An even more startling turnaround was displayed by Congressman Davis, a longtime foe of the Democratic party and a moderate Constitutional Unionist who seemed to favor the Republicans before and immediately after the election.[82] Known for his ambition and hopes of leading a combined Republican and Constitutional Unionist party in the South, Davis cast the pivotal vote for a distinctly Northern candidate in the protracted contest for Speaker of the House early in 1860.[83] Consequently, the congressman was censured by Maryland's general assembly for gross misrepresentation of the state's interests and feelings.[84] Davis was condemned in strong language by signed memorials from his constituents and burned in effigy throughout Maryland and the rest of the South.[85] He later reassured Marylanders that the interstate slave trade and slavery in the District of Columbia would be safe under Lincoln, and that the Republicans would enforce the Fugitive Slave law. When it became evident that Lincoln would deviate from the path that Davis had promised, the congressman became a bitter foe of the 'arch-Radical' president.[86]

Maryland cast her vote for the Southern Democrats and, like her sister state of Virginia, showed strong support for the conservative, pro-slavery Constitutional Unionists. This display of Southern conservatism unquestionably rejected Lincoln and his sectional party, which prevailed by a majority of electoral votes of the exclusively Northern states. Lincoln received 1,857,610 votes out of just less than 5,000,000 cast, which meant that less than four out of every ten men voted Republican.[87] Through its power in the electoral college, a minority of Republican voters in the North had elected a president that three million American voters had rejected.

The announcement of the Republican candidate's victory by vice-president John C. Breckinridge, later a U.S. senator from Kentucky and a major-general in the army of the Confederacy and secretary of war for the Confederate States of America, was greeted by the profound silence of the assembled Congress. Nor was the proclamation saluted by a single cheer from the multitude present in the capital. A sense that a wrong had been committed through legal constitutional procedure was felt in the North as well as the South.

Chapter Two

The Secession Winter

The Republican convention of May 1860 comprised official delegates from only seventeen states, all Northern.[1] The spirit of the gathering was sectional as ultras of several parties and of no party made their presence felt. There was disagreement and bickering on all policies except the one paramount plank which fired the party—sectional control of the government. Though denied by the Republicans, this attempt at sectional control was resented by all other parties who were themselves multi-sectional.

Lincoln's election by less than forty percent of the popular vote facilitated the subsequent subjection of the majority to the minority and, coupled with the neutralization of Southern voting power, constituted a slander on the national sense of propriety, fairness, and generosity. A minority of Northern voters benefitted from the state electoral vote under constitutional forms to acquire political ascendancy. The impetus behind this movement was the supposition that the Southern states possessed property under the same Constitution which ought not to be recognized.[2]

It was not Mr. Lincoln that the South stood against, but the domination of one section of the Union over another. The national conservatives, divided as they were among different parties, knew by October of 1860 that even a solid Southern vote for one candidate could not defeat the Republicans. This resignation in the South that their fate would be decided in the North exacerbated the feelings of helplessness and increased calls for secession by the supporters of Bell and Douglas as well as Breckinridge.

Despite Republican attempts to conceal the anti-slavery principles in its Chicago platform, informed persons North and South knew that Lincoln was supported by and would seek counsel from the sympathizers of John Brown, abettors to the likes of Jim Lane of Kansas infamy and opponents of the Fugitive Slave Law. The election of a strictly sectional candidate with that type of support could only lead to war.[3]

Maryland's responses to the Republican victory ranged from immediate calls for secession to a stated hope that the Union could be preserved by yet another compromise. The Baltimore *Sun* called Breckinridge's victory in Maryland, "an appropriate demonstration in defense of Southern Rights and institutions."[4] The *Sun* also accused Northern abolitionists of "practical disunion" by their repudiation of the Fugitive Slave law under the pressure of "an intolerant minority," and went on to list Northern violations of Southern rights. The Frederick *Herald* urged a serious, deliberate consideration of secession while the Centerville *Advocate* and the Patapsco *Enterprise* came out in favor of an immediate severance of Maryland's ties to the Northern states.[6]

Communities were alive with public meetings denouncing the Republican victory and calling for secession. Militia groups all over the state began to arm themselves against possible Northern coercion. One such meeting, held in Beantown, Charles County, requested all Republicans who had voted for Abraham Lincoln to leave the county by January 1, 1861. No logistical problems were encountered in complying with this "request" since only six voters in the entire county had thought it a good idea to elect Lincoln president.[7]

Northern abolitionists passed off threats of secession with the theory that once war began, "servile" insurrections would insure a speedy subjugation of the South. Non-partisan and conservative Northerners hurried to rebuke such theories about the butchery of Southerners by Negroes as monstrous. This debate highlights the Northern misconception of the relationship between slave and master in the South. As the war progressed, Northerners were surprised when the large majority of Negroes not only did not revolt but remained faithful to the Confederacy, evoking the generous spirit of the South.[8]

Public meetings were also held in the North as apprehensions of danger to the Union began to surface soon after the election. Statements produced at these mass meetings and those of eminent citizens held Southern fears as justifiable and called on non-partisan Northerners to work toward averting the impending crisis. Northern businessmen also began to call for compromise as imports of specie began to decrease, foreign and general inter-sectional trade fell off, and the national economy slowly slipped into recession. Business interests came out listing the great value of the South to the Union and to the trade of the North in general stating, "The North derives from forty to fifty millions revenue annually from Southern consumption through the tariff. The aggregate trade of the South in northern markets [winter 1860-61] was estimated at $400,000,000 every year."9 Even this show of temperance by large groups of Northerners could not dampen the disunion spirit fired as it was by attacks of the radical press. This offensive countervailed the conciliatory efforts of patriots everywhere. Northern moderates and Southerners sensed the futility of further attempts at compromise.

President Buchanan, never known as a great crisis leader, hamstrung by a badly split Democratic party, and with only four months left before the victorious Republicans would come sweeping into office, was hard pressed to deal with the problems of a nation on the threshold of civil war. Buchanan's cabinet, the majority being anti-secessionists, vacillated as to the proper course of action to hold the country together. Before the election, General Winfield Scott proposed to make secession impossible by moving troops to forts and garrisons in the South in an effort to pin that region to the Union with bayonets. This plan was rejected because it would have precipitated war before the election and would probably have resulted in the capture of the entire regular army. The administration finally settled on the policy of abandoning South Carolina to its avowed secession in the hope of confining the movement to that one state. However, the plan did call for the strengthening of federal positions in Charleston Harbor, a move which only further alarmed South Carolinians and justified their apprehensions.

Buchanan's speech to Congress on December 3, 1860, was conciliatory in nature. It gave hope to the South that a compromise could still be reached but stopped short of proposing strong legislation to insure maintenance of the Union. The Pennsylvania-born president began by asking why such a prosperous nation was now so discontent. In answer to his own query, Buchanan cited the "just complaint" made by the Southern people against the sectional legislation of the Northern states in the form of resistance to the Fugitive Slave Law. Buchanan continued by discussing solutions:

> All that is necessary to accomplish the object and all for which the slave states have ever contended is to be left alone and permitted to manage their domestic institutions in their own way. As sovereign states, they, and they alone, are responsible before God and the world for the slavery existing among them.10

The chief executive went on to censure the nullification laws of several
Northern states, called Personal Liberty bills. He said that the other states
had the right to demand their repeal, and if refused, the injured states,
due to violation by the enacting states of the Constitution in a "provision
essential to the domestic security and happiness of the remainder," would,
after having exhausted all "constitutional means to obtain redress, [be]
justified in revolutionary resistance to the government of the Union."[11]
Buchanan was, of course, severely criticized by the Northern abolitionist
press for this stance.[12]

The president labelled "coercion" of any seceding states as
"unconstitutional" in his speech, yet approved of the feverish work to
strengthen the federal forts in Charleston Harbor prior to the secession of
South Carolina, despite his assurance that there would be no change in
the military status of federal installations during the remainder of his
administration. By strengthening the forts and refusing to order Major
Robert A. Anderson, the federal commander in Charleston, back into
Fort Moultrie, Buchanan broke his pledge. Anderson acted on his own in
retiring from Moultrie to Fort Sumter, thereby concentrating his
previously strung-out forces in a stronger, more strategic position in the
middle of the ship channel. To the South Carolinians, any unauthorized
change was an act of coercion. A closer look at Anderson's movement,
though having the appearance and effect of a defensive retreat, shows that
it also presented the Union commander with strong offensive possibilities.
With the Union garrison concentrated in a directly unassailable
position—for South Carolina had no navy with which to attack a well
armed fort—it could train its guns on the city and interdict shipping to
this important harbor.

Not only did Buchanan refuse to reoccupy Moultrie, but attempted to
covertly reinforce Sumter in an operation disguised as a mercy mission to
reprovision a "starving garrison." When the federal steamship, *Star of the
West*, was driven off by South Carolina shore batteries before it could reach
Sumter, Buchanan acted surprised and injured. He tried to lessen the blow
by saying that his cabinet had concurred on the decision to reinforce the
fort. Jacob Thompson of Mississippi, then secretary of the interior, accused
Buchanan of slander, called the movement underhanded, a breach not
only of good faith toward South Carolina, but of personal confidence
between the president and his advisors, and left the cabinet in disgust.

On December 20, 1860, the same day that Major Anderson evacuated
Fort Moultrie, South Carolina acted without hesitation to exercise her
rights as a sovereign state and separate herself from the Union. Those in

the North who had scoffed at South Carolina's threats to secede were rudely surprised when, on the 9th of January 1861, Mississippi also seceded. Alabama and Florida followed by voting for secession on the 11th day of the same month, joined by Georgia on the 20th, Louisiana on the 26th, and Texas on the 1st of February. In the three months since the election of Lincoln, seven Cotton-Belt states had seceded and begun to seize federal military installations.

At the beginning of its session in December of 1860, Congress appointed committees to consider the state of the Union and work toward a compromise of the sectional crisis. In the House a "Committee of 33," one representative from each state, was appointed by the speaker. The committee was so weighted with Lincoln men and devoid of National Democratic representation from the Northern states that no serious result toward compromise was expected.[13] This was the same Speaker of the House for whom Maryland congressman Henry Winter Davis cast the pivotal vote early in 1860, thereby inviting censure upon himself from the state legislature.

John Crittenden of Kentucky, a member of the Senate's "Committee of 13," proposed a compromise plan that was both fair and conciliatory. The Crittenden Compromise called for the prohibition of slavery in all territories north of the line 36° 30'; the allowance of slavery south of that line, but requiring admission of states with or without slavery as the constitution of new states may provide; the prohibition of Congress to abolish slavery in any place within the limits of the slave states, or in the District of Columbia as long as it existed in Maryland or Virginia; payment to owners of runaway slaves where restoration was prohibited; and expressly reaffirmed that Congress had no power to interfere with slavery in the states. Considering the then current trends, Crittenden's plan, had it become policy, would in all probability have resulted in every territory becoming a free state, with the single exception of New Mexico.[15]

The Crittenden Compromise had the overwhelming support of all parties in Maryland,[16] and kept alive hopes across the nation that war could yet be averted. Hope turned to despair when the five Republican senators on the committee repeatedly opposed any compromise and substituted resolutions calling for no concessions of any kind, stating that the demands of the South were unreasonable and declaring that the remedy for the present dangers was simply to enforce the laws.[17] From this one can only conclude that abolitionist Republicans, in spite of conciliatory gestures from all sides, were in favor of using force to coerce the Southern states. President Buchanan later wrote:

> Had Congress thought proper to refer the Crittenden
> Compromises to the people of the several States, no
> person who observed the current of public opinion at the
> time, can fail to believe ... it would have received their
> approbation. Memorials in its favor poured into Congress
> from all portions of the North, even from New England.[18]

In fact a movement within the Senate calling for a "direct vote upon
the resolution, so earnestly desired by the country" was defeated by the
"parliamentary tactics of the Republican party." Thus the Republicans
persisted in their Chicago platform scheme and "terminated every
reasonable hope of any compromise between the North and the South."
This message was clearly understood in the South and naturally led to
further ill feelings and secessions.

The pivotal border slave states of Virginia, Maryland, Kentucky and
Missouri did not make their decisions in the secession winter of 1860-61
without help. In December, the first of a series of emissaries from Cotton-
Belt states arrived to see Governor Hicks. Hicks refused to recognize them
officially, but through important acquaintances these emissaries were able
to speak publicly and were warmly received by Maryland citizens.[20] Soon
thereafter a commission from Pennsylvania arrived to propose action by
states astride the Mason-Dixon line that would lead to further conciliatory
negotiations. Marylanders, in turn, some with commissions from the
governor and some without, travelled to Washington, D.C., Montgomery,
Alabama, and states throughout the North in an effort to promote talk of
compromise.[21] As it turned out, actions out-paced talk.

Like the citizens of other Southern states during that momentous
winter, Marylanders were anxious to insure defense of their political,
economic and social rights. In response to Governor Hicks's refusal to call
the general assembly into session, a meeting was held in Prince Georges
County in January of 1861. The delegates resolved that if Hicks did
nothing by the tenth of the month, then the speaker of the House of
Delegates and the president of the Senate would be justified in calling a
session of the legislature.[22] The plethora of local meetings in January of
1861 produced a "spontaneous combustion of frustration," which resulted
in a convention held in Baltimore on the tenth and eleventh of the
month.[23] All of the counties in Maryland and the city of Baltimore were
represented at this mass gathering that came out in favor of the Crittenden
proposals and urged Hicks to call for a referendum to decide on the need
for a state convention.[24]

On January 19th, the legislature of Virginia passed resolutions calling for a national Peace Conference to be held in Washington, D.C., on the 4th of February, with the purpose of reaching a negotiated settlement. The proposal received a favorable response in the border slave states, and the conference met on the appointed day with the venerable ex-president John Tyler of Virginia presiding. The delegation from Maryland, appointed by Hicks, was such a "cluster of colorless individuals that it excited considerable complaint" and inspired little confidence in the majority of Marylanders that their best interests would be served.[25] The plan adopted and presented to Congress on the 28th of February differed from the Crittenden plan in several features, but still favored the North.[26] Yet in vote after vote it was put down by the Republicans in both houses, whose refusal to compromise elicited bitter response from members of Congress in all sections. Whether or not the Confederacy would have been willing to compromise at this late date is unknown, but the determination to prevent settlement of difficulties by any concession on the part of the North was evident.

While the Peace Conference debated, a meeting was held in Baltimore on February 18. The talk was much tougher than in a similar meeting held on the 11th of January. The delegates met to answer the question: "what the honor and the interests of Maryland required her to do in the crisis." Resoundingly the answer came back: "Honor first—interest last."[27]

The extreme Southern party, led by young men such as Bradley T. Johnson, described the meeting as "such a demonstration of physical strength, of resolute purpose and of intelligent design,"[28] that calls for immediate action abounded. But desirous of staying within the bounds of the state constitution, the meeting resolved to urge Hicks once again to call for a state convention. The gathering adjourned until March 12th in order to give the governor time to act and to confront him with a deadline.[29]

The struggle to call the state legislature into special session had at first been fought within the framework of partisan politics. Hicks and the new American party naturally did not want the resurgent Democrats to be able to legislate in special session on any issue. But as the secession of the lower South proceeded and the inauguration of Lincoln grew near, a large majority of Marylanders anxiously called for steps to be taken in defense of their rights. Early in March a meeting in Frederick urged citizens to take matters into their own hands if Hicks refused to call the legislature. The people were urged to "act for themselves for the preservation of their rights."[30] By mid-month, sentiments for a "people's assembly" had spread statewide. Convening in Baltimore on the 12th, the delegates insisted that the governor no longer represented the feelings of the state and urged the formation of a "sovereign convention."[31] The convention resolved that if Hicks, who was trying to maintain good relations, as far as possible, with all sides, did nothing, and Virginia was to secede, then the conference convention would reconvene "with a view toward recommending to the people of the State, the election of delegates to such a Sovereign Convention."[32]

These actions appeared indecisive, but one must remember that Marylanders were responding to a number of then important exigencies and outside stimuli that they had no power to control. Besides a deep reverence for the Union and a desire, shared by all states, to continue the natural benefits of such a compact, there remained the hope that the seceded states could be brought back into the fold without bloodshed. The Southern Confederacy, which formed its government in February and March, spoke only of being left alone and had made no warlike advances on any other state in the Union. The federal army, beyond the posturing of General Scott at Lincoln's inauguration, had made no serious attempt to occupy Maryland soil nor transport troops across the state to subjugate the rest of the South. More importantly, Virginia, North Carolina, Tennessee, Kentucky, and Missouri had not yet decided whether to join the Confederacy or to stay in the Union. Maryland could not hope to secede if Virginia stayed in the Union, cut off as she was from the seceding states by her Chesapeake partner.

The Virginia legislature, shortly after its regularly scheduled meeting in January of 1861, called a convention to decide the proper course of action in its crisis with the Union. The election was held in the first week of February, and the majority of members voted against unconditional secession. As a result, Tennessee and North Carolina decided against calling secession conventions and, with Virginia and Maryland, awaited the results of national efforts to compromise.

While these events were transpiring, delegates from the seven seceded states were meeting in Montgomery, Alabama, to organize a new government. The Confederate constitution was adopted on the 8th of February and differed little from that of the United States. The president and vice president were to be elected for six years with no re-election. Jefferson Davis was inaugurated first president of the Confederacy on February 18, 1861, and speaking of the seceded states during the ceremony said, "In this they merely asserted the right which the Declaration of Independence of 1776 defined to be inalienable."[33]

"The Baltimore Plot," an alleged plan by Maryland secessionists to assassinate president-elect Lincoln on his inaugural journey to Washington, was an interesting episode that highlighted two very important variables in this strange drama of pre-war maneuverings in Maryland. It showed that the level of national hysteria and tension, already high and corruptive, continued to feed upon itself, particularly in Maryland. It brought out the true intentions of Maryland's governor, irrespective of public clamor, to hold the state in the Union by any means.

Lincoln's inaugural procession had to cross Maryland as it traveled by railroad to Washington. The last scheduled stop of the procession before reaching the nation's capital was Baltimore, which also happened to be the only Southern city on its route. Allen E. Pinkerton, of the detective agency fame, informed Lincoln's party that a plot existed to kill the president-elect.[34] After sucessfully sneaking Lincoln into the capital, Pinkerton claimed that he had been hired by the Philadelphia, Wilmington and Baltimore Railroad because its owners feared for the safety of company operations if Maryland seceded from the Union.

When it was learned that Lincoln had taken a special train in the night, there was a reaction of surprise, which changed to shame and profound humiliation when the cause of the surreptitious entry was revealed. Lincoln was ridiculed as a coward and degraded in both the North and South for accepting an alleged conspiracy against his life as an excuse for the disgraceful secrecy with which he, the future chief executive of the country, made his way through one of its principal cities.[35]

American citizens, especially Marylanders, were insulted that they were accused of plotting murder to repair a political defeat.[36] The consensus of the Northern press was that "the Anglo-Saxon race were not assassins; least of all are they so in the United States of America." The affair elicited on almost all sides mingled expressions of incredulity, bitterness, and ridicule,[37] and in the South this could only be seen as another indication that Lincoln was the champion of its enemies. In the North, suspicion heightened that Maryland would soon join the Confederacy.

On the day the president-elect was supposed to arrive in Baltimore, a crowd estimated at fifteen thousand gathered at the Calvert Street station and greeted the train with shouts and threats. People called out for "the damned black Republican" to appear, but the train carried only Mrs. Lincoln and the children. The gathering grew indignant when it learned that Lincoln had eluded them. The future first lady and her party made their way fearfully through the throng, where they were pushed, shaken and occasionally insulted, but uninjured.[38] Lincoln later regretted that he had agreed to change his plans, saying to his friend and companion on the trip, Ward Lamon, "The way we skulked into this city [the capital] has been a source of shame and regret to me, for it did look so cowardly!"[39]

But the damage had been done. Two days after Lincoln's scheduled arrival in Baltimore, the Baltimore *Sun* wrote: "Had we any respect for Mr. Lincoln, ... [sneaking through Baltimore] would have utterly destroyed it."[40]

Governor Hicks, who up until this point had pacified each viewpoint he encountered with just the right amount of rhetorical balm, began to crack under the pressure brought on by his self-serving duplicity. In 1858, Hicks expressed fear of the growing population of free Negroes and referred to "Maryland's favorite scheme of colonization" as a remedy, and further stated that "Maryland . . . has refused to join with the misguided people of the Northern States in their assaults on slavery."[41] But during the winter of 1860-61, while most of Maryland's leading politicians were leaning toward ideas of secession, Hicks was making a career out of advocating caution.

Hicks, an Eastern Shore farmer and slaveowner, first Democrat then Whig and finally Know-Nothing, had been elected governor of Maryland in 1857 as a compromise candidate on the seventh ballot. A rather lackluster fifty-nine-year-old politician, Hicks owed his election to his party affiliation and the law which called for the rotation of the governorship among Maryland's three regions.[42] Near the end of his term, during the secession winter and without a functioning party behind him, Hicks used every ploy within his means to resist calling the general assembly into session because he knew that body would vote for secession.[43] He had not forgotten that in looking ahead to the coming crisis, the Maryland General Assembly of 1860 had resolved "that should the hour ever arrive when the Union must be dissolved, Maryland will cast her lot with her sister States of the South and abide their fortune to the fullest extent."[44]

The governor was bombarded from all sections of Maryland by pleas to call the legislature and threats to his well-being if he refused. Two Talbot County meetings connected the calling of the legislature with the declaration that Maryland was a Southern state.[45] A group of Harford County citizens urged the convening of the general assembly so it could call a convention specifically empowered to "entertain" the idea of seceding.[46] Pro-legislature and anti-Hicks resolutions were made by citizens in Frederick, and during a speech in Carroll County the captain of a militia company damned Hicks for his refusal to heed the call of responsible Marylanders.[47]

In response to demands for him to call a special session of the legislature, Hicks offered a confusing proclamation purporting to state his views. He condemned as strongly as ever evasions of the Fugitive Slave law and declared that he hoped never to live in a state where slavery did not exist. He then admitted advocating the possibility of a division of the country and the justice with which the South could demand this as a last resort, but he continued to recommend a policy of inactivity, which, if events continued unaltered,

Maryland State Archives
Enoch Louis Lowe

must ultimately lead to the opposite outcome of his stated wants. Hicks's policy of cautious inactivity of course won him flowing praise in Northern newspapers. He contended that he was expressing the will of most of his constituents, but the many public meetings in the state and Maryland's elected representatives thought and spoke otherwise.[48]

Hicks was so convinced of plots to kill the president-elect that a month before Lincoln's inauguration he delivered a written warning to the commanding officer of the naval academy. However, he would not divulge, despite repeated insistence, from whence he got the information for fear of drying up the source.[49] In testimony before a United States House of Representatives committee appointed to look into "hostile organizations," former-governor Enoch Louis Lowe of Maryland "denounced Hicks as being responsible for many of the wild rumors then in circulation."[50] After first refusing to testify before the committee, Hicks finally relented but was able to add little to what was already known, "since publicity would prevent further opportunities of acquiring information."[51]

Once Lincoln was safely in Washington, Hicks consulted with the president personally and often concerning cabinet appointments and the crisis in Maryland. Already a hated man, Hicks's friendliness to the incoming administration brought him nothing but ridicule and open opposition. Marylanders resented the implied meaning of Hicks' refusal to call the legislature, that they were not capable of being entrusted with

a serious duty. One prominent citizen wrote of Hicks: "His conduct is that
of an oppressor; and if the people of Maryland longer submit to it, they
are, in my humble opinion only fit to be oppressed."[52] Speaking at the
convention held on February 18th in Baltimore, state representative
Severn Teackle Wallis, the chairman of the House Committee on Federal
Relations, stated that Hicks's very distrust of the legislature was good
reason why the citizens of the state should have confidence in that body.[53]
Another speaker suggested that Hicks be hanged.[54]

Many Marylanders accused Hicks of spreading rumors about the plan
to assassinate Lincoln in an attempt to alarm the new administration. It
was argued that the fear caused by such talk would certainly goad the
president into bringing more Northern troops down for the protection of
the capital and thereby ensure that Maryland would not dare to secede.
This may have been true, but as events proved, Lincoln needed no goading
to call for troops. No arrests were ever made in conjunction with the
alleged plot, and Lincoln's advisors later accused Pinkerton of fabricating
the whole story to get publicity for his agency.[55]

Near the end of March, Hicks became so confident of his strategies that
he covertly applied to General Scott for arms and soldiers, if these "should
become necessary to put down rebellion in this state"—all this when
military companies across Maryland were forming for the defense of the
state from Northern coercion. Hicks feared that if Virginia seceded there
would be a similar and immediate movement in Maryland. These talks
were held in the utmost secrecy, for if the public sensed that Hicks was
requesting federal troops to be used against Marylanders, his life would
have been in grave danger.[57] Bradley Johnson, then chairman of the
Democratic State Committee in Maryland, said of Hicks during these
times:

> He knew that Maryland was as ardently Southern as
> Virginia. He was a shrewd, sharp, positive man. He knew
> what he wanted and he took efficient means to procure
> it. He wanted to save Maryland to the Northern States.
> He believed the Union was gone. In the Southern
> Confederacy, Maryland must, in his opinion, play a
> subordinate part and he, himself, fall back into the
> political obscurity from which he had been recently
> raised. With the North, Maryland in possession of the
> national capital, protected by the Northern navy through
> her bay and great rivers, would be a conspicuous power,
> and he, as her governor, would fill a distinguished role.[58]

Had it been known that Hicks was trying to keep Maryland "quiet until she could be occupied by Northern troops and delivered, tied and manacled, to the Union authorities,"[59] he would have been viewed as a traitor and a saboteur and certainly expelled if not killed.

Four days after Lincoln's inauguration, Martin Crawford and John Forsyth, commissioners from the Confederate States, waited upon officials of the new administration to discuss the adjustment of existing difficulties upon terms of "amity and good will."[60] Secretary of State William H. Seward of New York refused to meet the commissioners personally, but gave assurances, through Supreme Court justice John A. Campbell, a well-disposed and patriotic third party, that plans were under way for the evacuation of Fort Sumter. In reality, preparations were being made in New York Harbor for a naval and military expedition against Charleston. Seward, who later admitted to the deception in glowing terms, had duped the Confederates into abstaining from action on an issue about which they had already been dealt with in bad faith. By the 8th of April the commissioners realized Seward's treachery and indignantly reproached him. They called attention to their earnest and ceaseless efforts in behalf of peace and placed the responsibility for the blood and mourning that may ensue on those who practiced treachery and who would deny the fundamental doctrine of American liberty that governments derive their just powers from the consent of the governed.[61]

Succumbing to the clamor of the radical element in his party, Lincoln had ordered the outfitting of the naval expedition to reinforce Sumter. But what would this do to the status quo? Was the retention of one fort and the remote possibility of controlling one Confederate city worth throwing away any current or future chance at compromise when seven states had already seceded and a warlike act such as this would most likely cause the secession of others? No. It seems more likely that the administration, pressured as it was to coerce the South, would welcome the inevitable first shot being fired by the Confederacy. In spite of the "advice of experienced and able military officers as to the futility of the attempt to reinforce Sumter by the employment of a few vessels," the politicians pressed on, believing a first shot by the South "would be worth the cost of the expedition and the destruction of a fleet."[62]

The knowledge of Seward's deceit and the presence of the federal fleet outside of the ship channel signaled the call to action in Charleston. At half-past four o'clock in the morning, on the 12th day of April, 1861, the bombardment of Sumter began. The federal fleet was unable to reach the fort due to rough seas and the work of Confederate shore batteries. Firing

on both sides continued until the afternoon of the following day, when
Major Anderson, his fort in ruins and burning, agreed to an unconditional
surrender. General Pierre Gustave Toutant de Beauregard, commander
of Confederate forces in Charleston, offered Anderson the most
"distinguished marks of lenity and consideration: his sword was returned
... [and he and his] garrison allowed to take passage, at their convenience,
for New York."[63]

The time for talk had come to an end. Abolitionist pressure had created
a situation where no one could remain neutral. Northern moderates and
border slave state compromisers, where feasible, began to make
preparations for an inevitable military confrontation. The goal for which
the abolitionists had for fifteen years openly labored, the destruction of
the government and extinction of the Republic, was finally obtained.
Wendell Phillips, an activist in the American Anti-Slavery Society, put it
best in his speech at the Music Hall in Boston on July 6, 1862:

> The abolition enterprise was started in 1831. Until 1846
> we thought it was possible to kill slavery and save the
> Union. We then said, over the ruins of the American
> Church and the Union is the only way to freedom. From
> '46 to '61 we preached that doctrine.[64]

The New York *Tribune*, leading mouthpiece "of the advanced section
of the Republican party" had even come out in defense of the absolute
right of secession as late as November 9, 1860, stating: "Whenever any
considerable section of our Union shall deliberately resolve to go out, we
shall resist all coercive measures designed to keep it in."[65]

After the surrender of Fort Sumter, and in the light of Lincoln's call for
75,000 volunteers to coerce "combinations too powerful to be suppressed
by the ordinary course of judicial proceedings," there could be no more
talk in the North about letting the Southern states secede and no more
waiting and watching by Virginia and Maryland. Their choice was to join
the North to subjugate "sister Southern states," a policy statedly abhorrent
to the Tidewater partners, or resist the federal government and be
invaded. Virginia eventually seceded, but timing, geography and
circumstance robbed Maryland of all but the chance of offering token
resistance.

Chapter Three

The South's First Casualty

The southward movement of Northern troops, especially those from Massachusetts, began immediately upon Lincoln's call for 75,000 volunteers on April 14, 1861. Within days the regiments were approaching the borders of Maryland via the railroad. This move was viewed with suspicion in Maryland and raised two important questions. Was the movement of troops really to protect the as yet unthreatened capital or, as many Marylanders suspected, were they to take military control of the state and force it to remain in the Union? And should Maryland allow Union troops to cross over her territory to strike at sister Southern states or even to protect Washington?[1]

The pace of events accelerated in Baltimore on April 18th as city officials received word that two companies of regular United States artillery and four companies of unarmed Pennsylvania militia would pass through town that day en route to Washington. Mayor George William Brown, a "high minded, just and honorable gentleman . . . [but] a lawyer and an old man,"[2] sensed the possible dangers involved with such a passage of troops and issued a proclamation to Baltimoreans urging calm and the avoidance of provocative acts. When recalling the excitement produced in the citizenry by the threat of Northern invasion, Brown later wrote, "I cannot flatter myself that this appeal produced much effect."[3]

On April 18th, around 2:00 P.M., Northern troops under Major John Clifford Pemberton arrived via the Northern Central Railroad station on Bolton Street at the north end of town. The soldiers were escorted by a double file of 130 city policemen, led by police marshal George P. Kane. A howling throng, "who displayed secession flags" and cheered for "Jeff Davis and the Southern Confederacy,"[4] harried the troops as they marched down Howard Street toward the Baltimore & Ohio Railroad

Maryland Historical Society
George William Brown,
mayor of Baltimore

University of Alabama
George P. Kane,
police marshal of Baltimore

University of Alabama

Baltimore Uprising

station. It was not until the soldiers boarded the train for Washington that the crowd became unruly. A few of the more courageous civilians climbed atop the cars and pelted the troops with bricks as the train rolled southward to a chorus of "Dixie."[5]

News of Virginia's secession and the capture of Harpers Ferry by her troops, which included several companies of Marylanders commanded by Bradley T. Johnson, electrified the already excited residents of Baltimore. The Stars and Stripes was hauled down, even over the halls of Union clubs, and everywhere one could see the first national flag (also known as the Stars and Bars) of the Confederacy, the palmetto of South Carolina, and the Calvert banner of Maryland. The telegraph was alive with reports of troops converging on Baltimore from the north and west. There was no official notification of when and where these troops would arrive, perhaps due to Northern mistrust of city authorities.[6]

The waiting came to an end when thirty-five rail cars containing the Sixth Massachusetts Regiment rolled into the President Street station at approximately 11 A.M. on the 19th. Instead of marching in a body as planned, the troops remained in the cars, which were each pulled by four horses down Pratt Street at top speed. This aroused public suspicion, and when it became known that the troops were from Massachusetts, an abolitionist state, the movement became doubly offensive to the increasing number of infuriated men.[7] This so-called mob was composed of "[m]any prominent and respectable persons ... seeking to repel what they considered an invasion of Maryland."[8] Nine cars containing seven companies managed to reach the Camden Street Station, but "that was as much as human nature could bear."[9] The ninth car was attacked by angry citizens who hurled paving stones from a construction site near Gay Street. The people then began to obstruct the track with anything at hand, including anchors from the nearby dockyard. The drivers of the remaining cars were forced to stop, hitch the horses to the rear of their cars and pull the last four companies back to their starting point.

The Massachusetts troops then marched out of the President Street station, formed a column of fours and proceeded back down Pratt Street.[10] Encouraged by their earlier success, a dense mass of infuriated and excited men led by a color-bearer carrying a large Confederate flag, packed the street and sought to oppose the progress of the troops. The soldiers had to push their way through the crowd amid a hail of paving stones and cheers for Jefferson Davis and the Confederacy. Instead of halting and confronting their enemy, the rattled officers now ordered their militiamen to move at the double-quick. In the excitement, this pace turned into a ragged half-run. A pistol shot rang out, then two. The inexperienced soldiers turned and fired. The citizens dropped bleeding in their tracks, and the troops resumed their flight. At the sight of their dead compatriots, the crowd went wild.[11] Enraged men rushed upon the Northerners, wrenched muskets from the their hands and shot them down.

Mayor Brown, hastening from Camden Station to the scene of the melée, arrived near the Pratt Street bridge and placed himself next to Captain A. S. Follansbee, the commanding officer. Brown, now at the head of the column "with a gallantry and chivalry beyond imagination,"[12] and armed with only his furled umbrella, tried to lend an air of calm authority to the scene. He convinced Follansbee that the double-quick pace indicated panic and served only to further incite the crowd. The regular march order was given, but Brown also told the captain, "You must defend yourself."[13] The citizens of Baltimore respected and admired George William Brown, and "his escort of the invader was submitted to while he was present." But as soon as the head of the column passed, stone and shot began to pour in on the troops once more. Again they turned and fired, felling citizens at South Street and again at Light Street.[14] All reason fled as one man "jerked the sword out of the hand of an officer and ran him through with it,"[15] and others tore the Union flags from their lances. The people fell in clumps as the panicking soldiers fired without discipline or direction.

Having received word at the police station of the disturbance on Pratt Street, Marshal Kane hastily gathered fifty policemen and advanced on the scene at a run. The battle was raging furiously as Kane swung his officers in a line across the street behind the Union militia. The marshal drew his pistol and shouted, "Keep back, men, or I shoot!"[16] The crowd hesitated and stood back from attacking their own. With the mayor leading the way and the chief of police backed by fifty men with drawn pistols in rear, the battered Massachusetts militia made its way to Camden Station without further incident. But four soldiers were dead and some three dozen seriously wounded. Twelve citizens lay dying in the streets, and an undetermined number were injured.[17] The list of fallen Baltimore patriots was later increased by one when Robert W. Davis, a reputable and well-known citizen, was shot dead from the window of the train by a vengeful Massachusetts soldier. The dead man's crime and the alleged provocation had been a cheer for Jefferson Davis and the South.[18]

The people of Baltimore were outraged by the passage of troops and the citizens left dead in their wake. The mood of the city on the afternoon of the 19th was a volatile one. Barricades were thrown up across the railroad tracks leading through town, gun shops and armories were emptied of their weapons, and attempts were made to cut the telegraph wires to the North. Angry groups of citizens readied themselves for the arrival of more federal troops rumored to be converging on Baltimore. A telegram was sent to Lincoln in Washington by Mayor Brown and Governor Hicks informing the president of the disturbance and asking that no more federal troops be sent through the city. Brown firmly stated, "It is not possible for more soldiers to pass through Baltimore unless they fight their way at every step." Hicks implored, "The excitement is fearful. Send no troops here."[19]

The telegram went ominously unanswered.

The mood on the streets was so explosive that the mayor called a mass meeting to be held at 3:00 P.M. in Monument Square. In an attempt to quiet the crowd, Brown asked several well-known citizens, including Alexander C. Robinson, William P. Preston, Severn Teackle Wallis, and John E. Wethered, to speak.[20] Hicks was fetched from his nearby hotel room. At the sight of the governor, the crowd became disturbingly quiet. His life was certainly in danger at this moment, and he could not have helped but sense it. Hicks's policy of "masterly inactivity," so lauded by the Northern press and despised by Marylanders, many of whom had made threats against his life, had "bound Maryland until she was now helpless."[21] The battle on the 19th had so intensified these feelings against Hicks that had he dared "express himself in any way in opposition to the one will and purpose which dominated the crowd, the entire police force of the city present could not prevent his life from being taken."[22]

Standing next to the state flag, Hicks began by reiterating his deep desire to see the Union preserved. The crowd began to cry out in anger at this. Visibly shaken, Hicks announced:

> I coincide in the sentiment of your worthy mayor. After three conferences we have agreed, and I bow in submission to the people. I am a Marylander; I love my State and I love the Union, but I will suffer my right arm to be torn from my body before I will raise it to strike a sister State.[23]

Later actions and statements by Hicks indicate that he was either cracking under the pressure or lying when he made this proclamation. Sensing that others in the crowd questioned the faithfulness of Hicks, Brown invited the governor to spend the evening at his home. There were certainly grounds for fear of Hicks's safety if he returned to his hotel.[24]

Later that evening, at Mayor Brown's, an emergency meeting of city

University of Alabama
Burning of a railroad bridge on the Gunpowder River.

leaders was held in Hicks's bedroom because he was too stricken to stand. Those present vehemently denounced the federal administration for crossing troops over Maryland to be used against the seceded states. The earlier telegram imploring the government in Washington to send no more soldiers remained unanswered. City authorities had received word that Northern troops, vowing revenge on the "Baltimore mob,"[25] were en route from Philadelphia and Harrisburg. The telegraph also brought news of Northern newspapers clamoring for revenge. From Boston, the *Courier* urged Massachusetts men to "organize, arm and push on to Baltimore to lay it in ashes."[26] From New York, the *Herald* proposed that troops should "cut their way through Baltimore,"[27] and the slogan was repeated, "Through Baltimore or over it."[28] The prospect of prevailing upon Lincoln to honor public demand in Maryland was given little chance of success and it was decided by all present that prompt and drastic measures were in order if United States government troops were to be kept from crossing the state.[29]

It was agreed that the most expedient way to retard further invasion was to burn the railroad bridges to the north and east of the city. Later, when the federal grip was more firmly tightened upon Maryland, Hicks denied that he had given the order to burn the bridges.[30] The others present later stated—and historians are in agreement—that the governor did indeed authorize the demolition.[31] Around 2:30 A.M., an hour after consent was given, Maryland Home Guard troops and a detachment of Baltimore police, ably assisted by some private demolition teams, set the bridges afire and picketed the rivers.

That same evening a call was put out to the local military companies, who were standing at the ready, to converge on Baltimore. Marshal Kane telegraphed Bradley T. Johnson at Frederick: "Streets red with Maryland blood. Send expresses over the mountains of Maryland and Virginia for the riflemen to come, without delay. Fresh hordes will be down on us tomorrow. We will fight them and whip them or die."[32] Johnson and the Frederick company directly commandeered the moving train on the Baltimore & Ohio line, and by eleven o'clock were marching toward Monument Square. Soon after came two troops of cavalry from Baltimore County, followed that night by the Patapsco Dragoons from Anne Arundel County.

Early on Saturday, April 20th, an emergency meeting of the city council appropriated $500,000 for the defense of Baltimore. Within three hours a group of bankers, many of them former Unionists, furnished that sum to Mayor Brown.[33] Also on Saturday, the Garrison Forest Rangers, under the command of Captain Wilson Carey Nicholas, later Company G, First Maryland Regiment of Cavalry, Confederate States of America, seized the United States arsenal at Pikesville. The commander at Pikesville, Colonel Benjamin Huger of South Carolina, who had just resigned from the army of the United States, was made colonel of the Fifty-third Regiment, Maryland Militia, composed of the Independent Grays and the six companies of the Maryland Guard. The Fifty-third Maryland was ably drilled and officered, the majority of them later serving in the Confederate States Army.[34]

Later on the 20th, Mayor Brown issued a call for all citizens with arms to deposit them with the commissioner of police and for all those willing to enroll for military service to come forward. Fifteen thousand citizens stepped forward in defense of their state and organized that day under the command of Colonel Isaac R. Trimble, later major-general, CSA, who served with distinction under Jackson and Lee.[35]

In response to rumors that a group of citizens planned to attack the federal garrison in Fort McHenry, police commissioner John W. Davis called on the fort that evening to warn the commanding officer. He proposed that a contingent of the Maryland Guard be stationed outside the grounds. Knowing the Confederate sympathies of the Guard, the officer agreed, but declared that if attacked he would open fire on the troops and on the Washington Monument. He was referring to a well-known monument in the densely populated center of old Baltimore, an act which would certainly cause many civilian casualties. The discussion became violent, with Davis asserting that if the fort did fire into the town and a single woman or child should be killed, nothing would be left of the regulars but their brass buttons.[36]

Sunday morning, April 21st, saw the arrival of the Howard County Dragoons under Captain George Ridgely Gaither. Two companies arrived by boat from Easton, along with the news that the companies from Harford, Cecil, Carroll, Charles, Queen Anne's and Prince George's counties were on the march or preparing to move.[37] The mood was one of powerful anticipation, prompting Mayor Brown to describe the citizenry: "Women, children, and men, too, were wild with excitement."[38] Around half-past ten, two riders galloped up to city hall, shouting, "The Yankees are coming, the Yankees are coming!" The Yankees were twenty-four hundred Pennsylvania militia who had advanced as far as Cockeysville, not twenty miles from Baltimore. Bradley T. Johnson describes the effect of the news:

> These couriers of disaster brought the news of this fresh invasion and flashed through the city like an electric shock. The churches dismissed their congregations, their bells rang, and in the twinkling of an eye the streets were packed with people—men and women in the hysterics of excitement pressing guns, pistols, fowling pieces, swords, daggers, bowie knives, every variety of weapon, upon the [militia] and beseeching them to drive back the hated invader. In an hour Monument Square was packed, crammed with such a mass of quivering humanity as has rarely been seen.[39]

Earlier that morning Mayor Brown, accompanied by several prominent citizens, traveled to Washington at Lincoln's request to discuss ways to preserve peace. On the same day, U. S. Senator Anthony Kennedy and congressman J. Morrison Harris met with Lincoln, Seward, and Scott, independently of Brown's party.[40] The absence of Hicks, called to the meeting but hesitantly fumbling around in quiet Annapolis, added to the multiplicity of disconcerted action. Hicks certainly had no pressing business in Annapolis, but was merely waiting to see which side would prevail in the test of strength. All of this only further confused matters and in no way served the best interest of Marylanders, who continued to insist that no more troops should or could be sent across the state.[41]

Lincoln and the administration must have sensed the unpreparedness of Maryland officials for concerted action and their lack of understanding of the state's citizenry, who were in obvious revolt. The telegraph wires and railroads to the north of Baltimore were all cut, thereby isolating and endangering the capital for several days. State troops drilled daily in the parks of Baltimore while others marched toward the city. Telling each group what they wanted to hear, the president insisted that federal troops must pass over the state, but not through Baltimore, and that they were not to be used against Maryland, but only for the defense of the capital.

University of Alabama
Brigadier General Benjamin F. Butler
Commander of 8th Massachusetts

These meetings and "agreements" by Lincoln were only intended to buy time, for on Saturday, April 20th, he had already ordered Brigadier General Benjamin F. Butler, commanding the Eighth Massachusetts Regiment, to advance on the capital. Butler was instructed to move through Perryville, at the extreme northern end of the Chesapeake Bay, thence by boat to Annapolis and onward to Washington via the Elkridge Railroad.

Governor Hicks, who emerged from his bedroom on Monday the 22nd, acting in view of the "extraordinary condition of affairs," called for the convening of the legislature in Annapolis on the 26th.[42] Hicks was still trying to placate Marylanders and maintain a working relationship with Lincoln and General Butler, who merely batted him back and forth. Butler answered Hicks' protest of the landing in Annapolis with a scolding, while Lincoln sternly dismissed the governor's continued urging not to provoke bloodshed by forcing a way through Maryland.[43] Maryland citizens were aware of these snubbings and once again berated Hicks for allowing the state to be humiliated by her chief executive. After forbidding Butler to land, he then tamely gave in to mere written correspondence and made no attempt to use the state's forces at his disposal to block the Northern general's movement.[44] These were the last critical days when a coordinated movement by Maryland authorities, in conjunction with the forces of Virginia and the Confederacy, could have saved the state from the humiliation of occupation without ever striking a counter-blow.

The federal occupation began in earnest early on Monday, April 22, as General Butler, viewing Maryland as "hostile territory,"[45] rejected the

University of Alabama
The 8th Massachusetts Regiment repairing a railroad bridge destroyed by
Confederate sympathizers.

protests of Hicks and Annapolis mayor John R. Magruder, and led his
troops to the Annapolis railroad depot. There he broke into a locked
building, repaired a dismantled locomotive, and before the day was over
was moving toward Washington on the Elkridge line. The Eighth
Massachusetts, now joined by the Seventh New York, made steady
progress toward Annapolis Junction, repairing as they went the tracks and
bridges torn up by Maryland partisans. By the afternoon of the 26th the
Seventh had reached Washington by rail, and the Eighth patrolled the
line from Annapolis. There was now an uninterrupted route for federal
reinforcements and supplies, which began to pour into Maryland and the
nation's capital.

On April 27 the federal administration went so far as to establish the
"Military Department of Annapolis" under Butler, who received his orders
from Lincoln through Commander-in-Chief Scott. Butler was given broad
powers to put down any pro-Southern movement by Marylanders and, if
necessary, to suspend the writ of *habeas corpus*.[46] He spent some days in
strengthening his position and then on May 5th moved on and took
possession of Relay House, nine miles southwest of Baltimore, where the

Washington branch, joined the main line of the Baltimore & Ohio leading westward through Harpers Ferry. The soldiers now with Butler, the Eighth New York, the Sixth Massachusetts and Major Cook's battery of Boston light artillery, hurriedly fortified this strategic rail link. All trains going west and south were searched, and scouts scoured the countryside for men and equipment bound to aid the Confederacy.[47]

Maryland State Archives
James Ryder Randall,
Author of "Maryland, My Maryland"

An incident occurred about this time that accentuated the intense hostility to federal invasion held by the citizens in the state and that held by native born Marylanders throughout the country. On April 23rd, James Ryder Randall, a twenty-two-year-old Marylander teaching at Poydras College, Louisiana, read of the battle in Baltimore four days earlier in the New Orleans *Delta*. Randall burned with indignation as he read of the Northern invasion with its disregard for Maryland's hard-won states rights. He was further perplexed when he saw the listing of his good friend, Francis X. Ward, as one of the "mortally wounded" at the hands of Massachusetts troops. Ward, a young lawyer, was the first civilian to fall in the melée, but recovered to serve with distinction in the Confederate States Army.[48] Unable to sleep that night and inspired to action, the young poet and teacher wrote feverishly by candlelight a poem that was to become the most popular and stirring battle hymn of the Confederacy, "Maryland, My Maryland!" sung majestically to the German folk song of 1799, "O Tannenbaum!"[49]

> *The despot's heel is on thy shore,*
>   *Maryland!*
> *His torch is at thy temple door,*
>   *Maryland!*
> *Avenge the patriotic gore*
> *That flecked the streets of Baltimore*
>   *Maryland! My Maryland!*

Hark to an exiled son's appeal,
  Maryland!
My Mother State! to thee I kneel,
  Maryland!
For life and death, for woe and weal,
Thy peerless chivalry reveal,
And gird thy beauteous limbs with steel,
  Maryland! My Maryland!

Thou wilt not cower in the dust,
  Maryland!
Thy beaming sword shall never rust,
  Maryland!
Remember Carroll's sacred trust,
Remember Howard's warlike thrust,-
And all thy slumberers with the just,
  Maryland! My Maryland!

Come! 'tis the red dawn of the day,
  Maryland!
Come with thy panoplied array,
  Maryland!
With Ringgold's spirit for the fray,
With Watson's blood at Monterey,
With fearless Lowe and dashing May,
  Maryland! My Maryland!

Come! for thy shield is bright and strong
  Maryland!
Come! for thy dalliance does thee wrong,
  Maryland!
Come to thine own heroic throng,
Stalking with Liberty along,
And chant thy dauntless slogan song,
  Maryland! My Maryland!

Dear Mother! burst thy tyrant's chain,
  Maryland!
Virginia should not call in vain,
  Maryland!

She meets her sisters on the plain—
"Sic semper!" 'tis the proud refrain
That baffles minions back again,
    Maryland! My Maryland!
I see the blush upon thy cheek,
    Maryland!
For thou wast ever bravely meek,
    Maryland!
But lo, there surges forth a shriek
From hill to hill, from creek to creek-
Potomac calls to Chesapeake
    Maryland! My Maryland!

Thou wilt not yield the Vandal toll,
    Maryland!
Thou wilt not crook to his control,
    Maryland!
Better the fire upon thee roll,
Better the blade, the shot, the bowl,
Than crucifixion of the soul,
    Maryland! My Maryland!

I hear the distant thunder-hum,
    Maryland!
The Old Line's bugle, fife, and drum,
    Maryland!
She is not dead, nor deaf, nor dumb-
Huzza! she spurns the Northern scum!
She breathes! she burns! she'll come! she'll come!
    Maryland! My Maryland![50]

Reprinted in paper after paper throughout the South, the poem did not reach Baltimore until the end of May, when it was then secretly circulated among the population. Hetty Cary, a young Baltimore woman said to be

> then in the prime of her first youth, with a perfect figure,
> exquisite complexion, the hair that Titian loved to paint,
> a brilliant intellect, grace personified, and a disposition
> the most charming—she was the most beautiful woman
> of the day[51]—

later took the lyrics and along with her sister, Jennie, put them to music.

The song went through the city like wildfire. Children sang it as they played, and scarcely a gathering of Southern sympathizers could occur that the people did not burst into an emotion choked rendition. Nothing, including "all the power of the provost-marshal and the garrison and the detectives could still the refrain

> The despot's heel is on thy shore,
> Maryland!
> His torch is at thy temple door,
> Maryland!

for it was in the hearts of the people and it was true!"[52]

In December of 1861, after the storm had passed, Hicks sought to defend his April 22nd calling of the legislature. He stated that he had done so to forestall an unconstitutional convening of that body by secessionists in Baltimore. Hicks's answer to the accusation that he had not allowed Maryland to defend her honor by calling out the state militia was that he had tried, but finding that very many of the officers were "in league with the conspirators," he thought their presence would do more harm than good.[53] This statement and others like it clearly show Hicks's supercilious disdain for the feelings of Marylanders; for whom, other than himself and possibly the Massachusetts and New York militia, would the Maryland militia have harmed? Hicks finally summoned the legislature out of fear for his life, for his refusal to do so had been a constant menace to his personal safety.[54] Not only would the people have taken matters into their own hands in some extra-legal way, but Hicks would have lost even indirect control of policy in Maryland. By finally calling the legislature, Hicks was able to forestall action by the people in defense of their rights and maintain some control of events while continuing to negotiate personally with the federal government.

On April 24th, Hicks changed the meeting place for the legislature from Annapolis, then under federal military control, to Frederick. At the time Hicks said he made the change for the "safety and comfort of the members,"[55] but later bragged that he had made the switch due to what he believed was Union sympathy in that region of the state.[56] The governor, playing a shrewd and dangerous game, hurried through Baltimore to Frederick, ever conscious of the continued danger to his life from the ultra-Southern faction, a danger so real that the secretary of state, James Partridge, resigned his position rather than face the risks.

Hicks's pro-Southern, anti-Lincoln remarks on the 19th of April, and his movement of the general assembly to Frederick, implying that he wished that body to be free from the influence of United States soldiers in Annapolis, gained him some measure of acceptance from the more conservative legislators. Though viewed as an eleventh-hour man by Marylanders and ridiculed for his treasonous behavior by the Northern press, Hicks played up the impression that he was heart and soul with the friends of the South.[57] Playing for time, Hicks's opening message to the legislature denounced acts that would lead to further bloodshed and called for calmness and further deliberation. But in the same message, when speaking of secession, he mentioned the possibility in the future of Maryland "taking sides against the federal government."[58] For now Hicks recommended the policy of "armed neutrality," the absurd idea floated around by some in the border slave states that a state could remain in the Union yet refuse to participate in the war. Could anyone in his right mind believe that Lincoln, at the helm of the potentially vast Northern war-machine and sworn to wage war against the Southern states, would allow border slave states to remain neutral and respect their sovereignty?

With the state in the grip of the federal army, the conservative old lawyers in Maryland's House and Senate responded to a memorial from Prince George's County asking for the immediate passage of an act of secession by resolving that the legislature was constitutionally unable to comply with such a request. It was promised that a sovereign convention capable of voting on secession could be called in the future if the need became clearly evident.[59] Considering the recent events, what more evidence could these venerable old men have required?

Whether or not Maryland's legislators believed themselves lawfully unable, within the framework of the state constitution, to break with the Union, or, in light of the occupation, saw the futility and ruin of such action, the one clearly evident characteristic of their legislation during the special session was a pronounced opposition to the United States government. The actions of Baltimore authorities to halt the passage of troops through the city and the subsequent military defensive measures were approved.[60] The city's $500,000 defense loan was deemed to be legal, and the Ways and Means Committee of the House was asked to prepare a $2,000,000 defense bill for the state.[61] The suspension of specie payments by the state banks was justified, and sovereign measures were taken to empower Maryland and its banks to issue currency.[62] The legislature also made valid the commissions of several militia officers who were pronounced Southern sympathizers, and who had become technically disqualified for failure to observe certain regulations.

With the federal army in firm control near the middle of May, the time for military action on the part of Marylanders had definitely passed and with it the excitement and fervor in Baltimore. The city had cut the rail link to Washington, but at the same time cut itself off from the large majority of its trade with the North and South. Marylanders had been forced to play their hand too soon, and now events were proceeding at a pace beyond their control. Butler felt strong enough by the evening of May 13th to roll into Baltimore during a thunderstorm and seize Federal Hill. He immediately fortified this commanding position and pointed fifty heavy guns at the town.[63] The following day he issued a proclamation to the people of Baltimore stating bluntly that the laws of the United States would be enforced, all munitions of war heading south would be seized, militia companies would be disbanded, and the display of flags, banners or other devices representing the Confederate States would not be allowed.[64]

The armed forces of the United States, actually predominant in the state since the 26th of April, were now in absolute control of Maryland and everyone knew it. The Union gunboats having control of the bay and the great rivers emptying into it—the Patapsco, the Patuxent and the Potomac—along with the ever-increasing number of army units pouring across the borders, dominated all parts of the state.

In retrospect, there had never really been a time when Maryland could have struck a successful blow for independence from the United States. A look at the map showing Maryland's position relative to the rest of the Southern states reveals the isolation and futility of a secessionist movement before Virginia embarked on a real course of action. Virginia did not legally decide to move until May 23th, and that was only the beginning of the vast and time consuming effort to ready itself for war. By this time "Maryland was bound hand and foot to the Union by the overwhelming force of the army of occupation."[65]

After endless conferences and discussion the legislature realized that any armed resistance to federal authority would be useless at present. However, they courageously adopted the following report submitted by the House Committee on Federal Relations, Severn Teackle Wallis, Esq., chairman:

> Whereas, in the judgment of the General Assembly of
> Maryland, the war now waged by the government of the
> United States upon the people of the Confederate States
> is unconstitutional in its origin, purposes and conduct;
> repugnant to civilization and sound policy; subversive of
> the free principles upon which the Federal Union was

founded, and certain to result in the hopeless and bloody overthrow of our existing institutions; and,

Whereas, the people of Maryland, while recognizing the obligations of their State, as a member of the Union, to submit in good faith to the exercise of all the legal and constitutional powers of the general government, and to join as one man in fighting its authorized battles, do reverence, nevertheless, the great American principle of self-government, and sympathize deeply with their Southern brethren in their noble and manly determination to uphold and defend the same; and,

Whereas, not merely on their own account, and to turn from their own soil the calamities of civil war, but for the blessed sake of humanity and to arrest the wanton shedding of fraternal blood in a miserable contest which can bring nothing with it but sorrow, shame and desolation, the people of Maryland are enlisted with their whole hearts on the side of reconciliation and peace;

Now, therefore, it is hereby resolved by the General Assembly of Maryland, that the State of Maryland owes it to her own self-respect and her respect for the Constitution, not less than her deepest and most honorable sympathies, to register this, her solemn protest, against the war which the Federal government has declared against the Confederate States of the South and our sister and neighbor, Virginia, and to announce her resolute determination to have no part or lot, directly or indirectly, in its prosecution.

Resolved, That the State of Maryland earnestly and anxiously desires the restoration of peace between the belligerent sections of the country; and the President, authorities and people of the Confederate States having over and over, officially and unofficially, declared that they seek only peace and self-defense, and to be let alone, and that they are willing to throw down the sword the instant the sword now drawn against them shall be sheathed-

The senators and delegates of Maryland do beseech and implore the President of the United States to accept the olive branch which is thus held out to him, and in the name of God and humanity to cease this unholy and most wretched and unprofitable strife, at least until the assembling of the Congress at Washington shall have given time for the prevalence of cool and better counsels.

Resolved, That the State of Maryland desires the peaceful and immediate recognition of the independence of the Confederate States, and hereby gives her cordial consent thereto, as a member of the Union, entertaining the profound conviction that the willing return of the Southern people to their former Federal relations is a thing beyond hope, and that the attempt to coerce them will only add slaughter and hate to impossibility.

Resolved, That the present military occupation of Maryland being for purpose which in the opinion of the legislature are in flagrant violation of the Constitution, the General Assembly of the State in the name of her people does hereby protest against the same and against the arbitrary restrictions and illegalities with which it is attended, calling upon all good citizens at the same time, in the most earnest and authoritative manner, to abstain from all violent and unlawful interference of every sort with the troops in transit through our territory, or quartered among us, and patiently and peacefully leave to time and reason the ultimate and certain re-establishment and vindication of the right.

Resolved: That under existing circumstances it is inexpedient to call a Sovereign Convention of the State at this time, or to take any measures for the immediate organization or arming of the militia.[66]

This report was forceful and based on truth and logic, but, nevertheless, it was merely words on a paper. The federal government acted, and the legislature heroically passed pro-Southern, but useless, resolutions.

Earlier in May, those pro-Southern men capable of continuing the struggle militarily had given up on the now impossible task of taking Maryland out of the Union. They had begun to make their way across the Potomac, first marching in groups and later individually, despite attempts by the federal army to hold them in Maryland. Under pressure, Hicks had consented to call out the militia after the events of the 19th of April; but later, resuscitated by Northern bayonets, had refused to call them out because, he declared, "a large number of the members of these companies wanted to go into the service of the Confederacy, and were only holding back in the hopes that Maryland would secede."[67]

Captain Bradley T. Johnson had left Frederick with his company on the 8th of May bound for Harpers Ferry, where, after receiving permission from Colonel Thomas J. Jackson, he would rendezvous with Captain Turner Ashby and his troops of horse. Johnson wrote, "The State was aflame and a steady stream of gallant youth poured into the rendezvous at Point of Rocks and Harpers Ferry," so that by the 22nd of May, eight companies of infantry had been mustered into the service of the Confederate States.[68]

> Fly to the South, fly with men,
> In Richmond, there's a home for thee.[69]

General Butler, stationed in Annapolis, was at a loss for how to deal with "volunteer troops which are passing within six miles of me daily. I have been in doubt whether or not to stop them—[and] what we should do with them after we have detained them."[70] Butler was told to stop the war matériel, not the men, from heading south. Obviously Lincoln did not feel sufficiently strong enough yet to test the ire of Maryland's citizenry and legislature by interfering with the movement of men. By summer's end, federal authorities would imprison anyone attempting to directly or indirectly aid the Confederacy.

A considerable number of Marylanders rendezvoused at Richmond. The volunteer companies—the Baltimore City guard, the Maryland guard, and the Independent Grays—formed the nucleus of the first three regiments from Maryland mustered into the service of Virginia.[71] Thousands of young Maryland men who got through the lines "were scattered all over the Confederacy" as they "sought out their relations and kinsmen in nearly every regiment of the army."[72] In time these troops quite naturally wanted to form into regiments with their statesmen and see the Maryland flag fly alongside the other Southern banners, but administrative delays and the hesitation of Confederate commanders to part with the spirited young Marylanders slowed the consolidation process. Finally, in response to an idea promoted by the state's officers of field rank serving in the Confederacy and influences from the older gentlemen left at home, the Maryland Line was formed. By 1863, a considerable number of Maryland units were gathered together and served under the banner, made in Baltimore and secretly brought over by Hetty

Cary, inscribed "First Regiment Maryland Line."[73]

Realizing the futility of resistance to the federal government's policy as evidently planned for Maryland and the rest of the Southern states, the members of the legislature adjourned on the 14th of May. But not wishing to leave control of the state entirely in the hands of Governor Hicks, again confident and now openly siding with Lincoln, they agreed to meet from time to time. What they hoped to accomplish by re-convening on June 4th is not clear. The grip of the Northern army, if anything, would certainly not loosen. Not knowing what to do, the legislators gave themselves the option that if the oppression of the United States government became intolerable, the people of the state, acting through elected officials, could offer some semblance of resistance.[74] Of Hicks, historian George Radcliffe wrote in 1901, "After months of uncertainty, confusion and tumult, Hicks, very materially aided by the federal administration, had outplayed his opponents and was winning steadily."[75]

The same day the legislature adjourned, Ross Winans, a highly respected industrialist and delegate from Baltimore City, was arrested at Relay House by an officer of the United States Army acting without a writ from a civil magistrate.[76] Hicks, who happened to be present, tried without success to obtain the release of the prisoner. Winans was accused of high treason, no specifics were given, and he was incarcerated in Fort McHenry. A storm of bitter criticism erupted from Marylanders, and Winans was released shortly thereafter, but not before a promise was extracted from him not to extend assistance to the Confederacy.

Before the month of May was out, another such offensive incident occurred in Maryland that attracted nationwide attention. John Merryman, a prominent citizen of Baltimore County, was rousted from his bed by a squad of soldiers without a warrant and locked up in Fort McHenry. The following day, a Sunday, Roger B. Taney, chief justice of the United States Supreme Court and a Marylander, issued a writ of *habeas corpus* for Merryman. General George Cadwalader, commanding at Fort McHenry, was to produce Merryman the following day at district court. Cadwalader refused to release his prisoner, citing orders from Lincoln himself. Taney then ordered an attachment to issue against Cadwalader and sent a marshal to arrest the general and bring him before the court. Having superior force arrayed against him, the marshal was unable to perform his duties, and, subsequently, Taney was reduced to filing a written opinion on the case. In it he demonstrated beyond a cavil that under the Constitution the president had no authority at any time, under any circumstances, to suspend the writ of *habeas corpus*. He directed that

Lincoln receive the entire record of the case for his further information and actions.[77]

Taney, a nationally respected elder statesman whose career had spanned the life of the Republic, guessed that even he might not be safe from imprisonment, but courageously stood by his convictions about American law and the purpose of the writ.[78] To defend Lincoln, the United States Congress later simply changed or reinterpreted the Constitution, as it has done repeatedly since the time of the Civil War, to accommodate political necessity. In the trial of

University of Alabama
Marylander Roger B. Taney,
chief justice of the U.S. Supreme Court

strength between the law and force of arms, the law became silent.[79]

Just days before the legislature was to reconvene, Hicks implemented a process by which he hoped to literally disarm the people of Maryland from offering any united opposition to the federal administration. If any doubts still existed in the minds of Marylanders that Hicks was wholeheartedly in support of the military subjugation of the state to prevent it from joining the Confederacy, these must have been removed by the posting of the following order:

> State of Maryland
> Annapolis, May 30, 1861.
>
> To Col. E. R. Petherbridge:
>
> Sir: You are hereby directed to collect immediately all arms and accoutrements belonging to the State of Maryland and hold the same in safe keeping subject to my order.
>
> Thos. H. Hicks,
> Governor of Maryland[80]

In a time when the proliferation and individual ownership of modern arms was impractical due to the high cost and time consuming manufacture of such weapons, a virtually unarmed citizenry would be at the mercy of even a relatively small, but well-armed, body of troops. Hicks defended his move by asserting that the existence of armed military companies was a constant source of unrest in the state. No doubt they were unsettling to him as well, considering that the companies, in the main, were in sympathy with the Confederacy.[81]

By law Maryland had two main armories, one in Frederick and one at Easton. Once the arms that had not already been sent south to aid the Confederacy were collected, Hicks displayed even more deceit and treachery. The arms at Easton were removed to federally controlled Fort McHenry, where they would be beyond the grasp of pro-Southern citizens on the Eastern Shore. To further overawe the legislature, Hicks distributed a portion of the arms held in Frederick to the somewhat irregular associations of Union sympathizers then descending on the town.[82]

The governor had confiscated arms from lawful militia companies and redistributed the weapons to what amounted to a political mob, a mob that intended to pressure the duly elected legislature with weapons purchased out of state funds and confiscated from patriotic citizens. These events highlight the absurd situation that most Marylanders were subjected to by having a governor working at cross-purposes to their wishes and a federal government promising restraint while pouring troops and materiél into the state with intent to subjugate.

On June 4 the legislature reconvened in Frederick and on the following day called upon Hicks to explain his bitterly criticized actions concerning the confiscation of state arms.[83] In a defiant reply, Hicks denied the right of the Senate or House to ask him such questions, but then proceeded to give a contemptible answer which in no way fulfilled the legislature's request.[84] Backed by the military arm of Lincoln, Hicks no longer feared any serious trouble from the legislature and impudently continued to insist that his actions were approved by his constituents. The remainder of the session was accentuated by the bitterness with which the legislature condemned Hicks and Lincoln, as well as the complete lack of cooperation between the governor and the rest of Maryland's elected officials.

On June 21, the Senate of Maryland harshly insulted Hicks, referring to his collection of state rifles a "palpable usurpation of authority" and called him a "military despot." It was demanded that Hicks confine himself to "the powers and duties confided to him by the constitution and the laws" and return the weapons to the military companies from which they had been taken.[85] Of course, Hicks took no action on this demand or on other inquiries about what he proposed to do "to protect the citizens of the state" from unlawful arrest by the federal army.[86] Not concerned over the citizens' plight but only with keeping power, Hicks, in a letter to General Robert Patterson, requested that a detachment of Pennsylvania troops be sent to Frederick—a request which the commander promised to fulfill.[87] The reasons given by Hicks for this request were to guard against attack by "rebels at Harpers Ferry," and to stop the sending of supplies from the temporary state capital to the South, the first being a very suspect assertion that only increased the contempt held for Hicks.[88] To the house's inquiry concerning the unlawful arrests of Maryland citizens, Hicks rather pompously retorted that he had been given no "official information" of these arrests, nor had the persons detained complained to him; therefore, he would take no action. The House sarcastically responded that the governor hardly need be "officially" told of arrests that attracted the attention of the entire country and involved a condemnation of the president and scathing opinion from the chief justice of the United States.

Not only did the attitude of the legislature toward the federal government become more and more hostile, but marked expressions of friendliness for the Confederacy increased. The legislature declared:

> The unconstitutional and arbitrary proceedings of the Federal executive have not been confined to the violation of the personal rights and liberties of the citizens of Maryland, but have been extended into every department of oppressive illegality, so that the property of no man is safe, the sanctity of no dwelling is respected, and the sacredness of private correspondence no longer exists; and,
>
> Whereas, the Senate and House of Delegates of Maryland, recognizing the obligations of the State, as far as in her lies, to protect and defend her people against usurped and arbitrary power, however difficult the fulfillment of that high obligation may be rendered by disastrous circumstances, feel it due to her dignity and independence that history should not record the overthrow of public freedom, for an instant, within her borders, without recording likewise the indignant expression of her resentment and remonstrance;
>
> Now, therefore, be it resolved, That the senate and house of delegates of Maryland, in the name and on

behalf of the good people of the State, do accordingly register this their earnest and unqualified protest against the oppressive and tyrannical assertion and exercise of military jurisdiction within the limits of Maryland, over the persons and property of her citizens, by the government of the United States, and do solemnly declare the same to be subversive of the most sacred guarantees of the Constitution and in flagrant violation of the fundamental and most cherished principles of American free government.[89]

Concerning secession of the Confederate States it was further resolved:

That the right of separation from the Federal Union is a right neither arising under nor prohibited by the Constitution, but a sovereign right independent of the Constitution to be exercised by the several States upon their own responsibility.[90]

Soon after these resolutions were passed, an unsuccessful attempt was made by a number of members to secure an adjournment *sine die*, and the legislature adjourned on June 25. The session was nearly as devoid of meaningful legislation as the previous one had been, but it was decided to meet again on the 30th of July. Days before this scheduled meeting, Marshal Kane, and later the police commissioners in Baltimore, were arrested by army forces.[91] Other arrests were made without restraint, and both public and private property was searched in a vigorous manner.

Marylanders had hoped that the United States Congress, which met on the 4th of July, would pass legislation aimed at the restoration of national peace. These hopes were crushed when early in the session Congress spurned any attempts at further compromise and continued the forceful prosecution of the war. If not for the time it took the Maryland legislature to refuse to fly the United States flag over the temporary statehouse in Frederick, consider memorials protesting the arrest of Marshal Kane, and pass further resolutions protesting the actions of the federal government, it might have adjourned the first day.[92] As it happened, the legislature assembled on July 30, and the session lasted a week. Before adjourning, the members tirelessly decided to meet once again, on September 17.

Following the Confederate victory at Manassas on July 21, 1861, the Lincoln government feared more than ever that Maryland would rise and secede from the Union. Though frantically gathering forces for the defense of Washington, the administration deemed it inadvisable to weaken the garrison in Baltimore. U.S. Secretary of War Simon Cameron issued the following order to General Nathan P. Banks:

> General: The passage of any act of secession by the Legislature of Maryland must be prevented. If necessary, all or any part of the members must be arrested. Exercise your own judgement as to the time and manner, but do the work efficiently.[93]

Banks needed no other prodding, and before the legislature could meet again, the army authorities moved. They arrested members and employees of the legislature across the state between the 13th and 17th of September. Squads of troops seized about thirty in Baltimore and Frederick alone, while imprisoning Mayor Brown, Frank Key Howard, editor of the Baltimore *Exchange*; Thomas W. Hall, editor of *The South*; Elihu Riley, editor of the Annapolis *Republican*; and Henry May, a Maryland representative in the United States Congress. The list included a number of citizens in all parts of Maryland charged with recruiting for the Confederacy or planning to join the Southern forces. None of these men were granted trials, and some were held in federal dungeons as long as fourteen months.[94] The gallantry of Mayor Brown and Marshal Kane in defending badly-officered federal troops on the 19th of April was rewarded by fourteen months in prison.

Southern sympathy in Maryland prior to the federal crackdown must have been much more substantial than has been recorded. Knowing that the most capable element opted for service with the Confederacy and those left behind were naturally vigorously suppressed by the Union army, it is understandable that Southern sympathy was not openly proclaimed in what amounted to a conquered military district.[95] Besides being saddled with a treacherous governor and being geographically vulnerable to Northern invasion, the blame for Maryland's inability to express her true will must rest with the leadership. Her legislators were brave, high-minded, and patriotic men, but were "dominated by the spirit of conservatism ... [and could not] understand how anything can be right which is unlawful, nor any process expedient or necessary which is illegal."[96] Unable to see that they were in the midst of a revolution, they counted on their constitutional rights. They talked of constitutional guarantees, of *habeas corpus*, trial by jury, free speech and law "until they and their constitutional guarantees were landed in Fort Lafayette or the military prisons in New York and Boston." Even then they continued to

"Costume of a Rebellious Woman" depicts dress of Confederate-sympathizing
Maryland women who flaunted this attire in the face of the army of occupation in
spite of laws to the contrary.

"protest that they could not be imprisoned without warrant, nor held
without bail," when all the while their homes were being invaded, their
state occupied, and their nation and institutions changed forever. They
may have been right in doctrine, but they were imprisoned and held
without recourse.[97]

While the legislature debated, more men headed southward, and the
women and children and those too old for military service patriotically did

what they could to aid the Confederacy. The recruiting of Confederate troops in Baltimore, conducted in the city since the time of South Carolina's secession, continued clandestinely but unabated. Prominent citizens, posting broadsides on private homes, courthouses, and trees, urged the formation of a Maryland Line for what would become Lee's Army of Northern Virginia.[98] The older men manufactured pikes and cast cannon; some raised the Confederate flag and used envelopes engraved with "Our Destiny is with the South" and "Jefferson Davis, why don't you come?" Of the women and youngsters it was written:

> All over the State, the women, irrepressible as ever in times of excitement, flaunted the Confederate red and white in the faces of the army of occupation. The babies wore red and white socks, the girls red and white ribbons —with red and white bouquets at their girdles and on their hearts, the young lads red and white cravats.[99]

One outstanding example of the patriotism shown by Maryland women for the Confederacy occurred late in May of 1861. The Maryland troops at Harpers Ferry who had rushed off enthusiastically to fight for the South were in a bad way. With their state occupied by federal troops, it became difficult to properly supply them with the implements of war. There was plenty of food, and the Virginia troops unselfishly shared other necessities, but what of arms and war supplies? Mrs. Bradley T. Johnson, "then in the prime of her youth, handsome, graceful, and accomplished," who with her little boy of five had left her comfortable home in Frederick to follow her husband, volunteered to help. Accompanied by two Maryland officers, she travelled to her ancestral home in North Carolina to wait upon her father and other illustrious citizens for aid. Simply, and in as few words as possible, she petitioned:

> Governor and gentlemen, I left my husband and his comrades in Virginia. They have left their homes in Maryland to fight for the South, but they have no arms, and I have come to my native State to beg my own people to help us. Give arms to my husband and his comrades, so that he can help you![100]

Her plea was met with a resounding cry of enthusiasm for the cause of the Marylanders. "Madam, you shall have everything that this state can give." At a time when every state in the Confederacy was straining to supply its own volunteers with arms and equipment, North Carolina instantly gave five hundred Mississippi rifles, ten thousand cartridges, and a liberal contribution of money with the words:

> If great events produce great men—so in the scene before us we have proof that great events produce great women. It was one that partook more of the romance than of the realities of life. One of our own daughters, raised in the lap of luxury, blessed with the enjoyment of all the elements of elegance and ease, had quit her peaceful home, followed her husband to the camp, and leaving him in that camp, has come to the home of her childhood to seek aid for him and his comrades, not because he is her husband, but because he is fighting the battles of his country, against a tyrant.[101]

Mrs. Johnson's return journey was one continued ovation as people, troops, and officials turned out at every stop, applauding the woman who was arming her husband's regiment and offering aid. After an absence of just ten days, she delivered to her husband the ample results of her energy, devotion and enthusiasm.

Nevertheless, while these pro-Southern events were taking place, the Union army completed its takeover of the state. As summer turned to fall, the disarming of the public, the suppression of the legislature, the arrests of prominent citizens, the suspension of some newspapers, and censorship over the remainder completed the process by which Maryland was brought almost completely under the control of the federal administration. Strategic points across the state, such as railroad bridges and canal locks, were under a permanent Union guard. Gunboats and other smaller Union craft patrolled every bridge and ford across the Potomac River, keeping a constant watch on Maryland's shoreline. The sprawling federal military camps spread into Prince Georges and Montgomery counties. The United States Naval Academy was moved to Rhode Island for the remainder of the war, and a large prisoner of war exchange installation, Camp Parole, was built just west of Annapolis. A large camp was later erected in Benedict, Charles County, for colored troops hurriedly enlisted near the end of the war.

Many public buildings and large tracts of land were commandeered to quarter strong Union detachments in Hagerstown, Clarysville, Cumberland, and throughout the Eastern Shore and southern Maryland, but despite the strong Union presence these areas were never completely brought under federal control. Open and continuous lines of communication to the South were maintained by Confederate sympathizers.[102] Crucial medical and military supplies reached the Confederacy on swift bay craft or in rowboats that routinely ran the Union blockade. Recruits for the Southern forces and correspondence found their way across the river, as did an occasional Confederate veteran visiting family in Maryland during a lull in the fighting.[103] Many of these adventurous and sometimes romantic stories are lost to history. As Maryland went through Reconstruction after the war, people did not write about these episodes for fear of punishment. What became known as "running the block" was an ongoing and dangerous business. Those unlucky enough to be caught by the Union pickets were imprisoned at Point Lookout, where they were carelessly treated and many died.[104] Military rule was harsh in Maryland; there was a strict enforcement of the decree forbidding the display or sale of Confederate photographs, flags, music, songs or badges.[105] To the majority of Marylanders, "the despot's heel is on thy shore" had a real and lasting meaning that subsequent events and writings have obscured.

Historians who speak of constitutional rights when defending the actions of the Northern states in the era of the Civil War must first be capable of ignoring many hard facts and of stretching small points to the limits of credulity. Let us put aside for a moment the argument over the "inalienable" right of self-government and a state's right to secede,[106] ably debated by many, yet not backed up militarily since the American Revolution and, therefore, not successfully proven by anyone in modern times.

To begin to speak of constitutionality in the era of the Civil War, one must first look to the forceful suspension of the hard-won rights of Marylanders held in the Bill of Rights of the U.S. Constitution. The suspension of freedom of speech; the suspension of the right to bear arms, a right which Jefferson knew would be indispensable in a people's fight against the establishment of a tyrannous central government; the illegal quartering of troops; unlawful search and seizures; the suspension of due process and the right to a speedy and public trial by impartial jury; and confinement without bail in Maryland—all show that from beginning to end the Lincoln administration had replaced the idealism of constitutional government with raw power politics for the subjugation of an entire continent.

Even modern authors like Jean H. Baker, William J. Evitts, and others who labor at stretching these points feel compelled to admit, reluctantly but without question, that the federal administration's decision to send troops through Annapolis prevented Maryland from seceding and that another clash in Baltimore would have propelled the state out of the Union.[107] Considering all the facts presented by the contemporaries and the course of events acknowledged by historians of the subject, it seems unavoidable to conclude anything other than that Maryland was held in the Union against her will at the point of a bayonet.

Still hoping for a compromise, wishing to avoid further bloodshed, and understanding their state's geographic vulnerability to invasion and isolation from the rest of the South, Maryland's elected officials struck deals with the Lincoln administration early on, which allowed Northern troops safe passage to the capital. Lincoln guaranteed that these troops would not be used against Maryland or the South; that turned out to be a lie. Once the troops were in Maryland, they took control of the state and within ninety days were marching into Virginia, bent on conquest. In these first weeks following Lincoln's inauguration, it was too early for the South to rise and assist Maryland. Virginia did not officially decide on secession until May 23, 1861, and, like the rest of the new Confederacy at this point, was too busy with internal matters to concentrate on issues outside her borders.

Through the fog of war, politics, and military preparations, there was talk in the South of helping Maryland, but there was no one man to rise up and take advantage of the possibilities presented. It seems that except for a small number of insightful or highly placed citizens, the public was not certain there would be outright war until the United States Congress met on July 4, and spurned all attempts at further compromise. The facts leave no doubt that the people in Maryland had risen in defense of their rights and for the South, but the timing in relation to the other Southern states was wrong. Maryland was forced to move too early by the mass of Northern militia pouring into the state by rail and on steamer. The treacherous actions of Governor Hicks combined with the shrewd political manipulation of events by Lincoln had prevented the citizens of Maryland from expressing their will. For the so-called "Unionists" in Maryland, who believed in the original compact between the states and in the Constitution but who demonstrated a marked revulsion to the federal administration's policy of coercion, and for the so-called "ultra Southern sympathizers," it was too late for action. The smallest protest was cause for arrest as the iron hand of federal military rule closed around the throat of the "Free State." As it was ably put by a Marylander of foresight and action, "Maryland thus suffered 'the crucifixion of the soul,' for her heart was with the Confederacy and her body bound and manacled to the Union."[108]

Chapter Four

The Trampled Ballot

Though most of the more ardent Southern-sympathizers were already south of the Potomac and the Union army controlled Maryland, the federal administration was still uneasy over the political intentions of the state's citizens. As the November election drew near in the fall of 1861, the United States government and its army took steps to guarantee a sweeping Union victory at the polls in Maryland.

General John A. Dix, commander of the military district, issued a proclamation which in essence forbad from voting anyone who had shown opposition to the federal government. Armed Union troops patrolled the areas about the polls and arrested "known Southern-sympathizers."[1] The following report written by a Pennsylvania colonel on November 8, 1861, is an example of the measures taken even in Western Maryland:

> Previous to the election a number of enemies to the Union in this State 'preliminated' schemes for disturbing the peace of the various precincts. I had several of the most prominent actors in this, among whom was a candidate for senator, arrested before election and held until to-day. I had 'detailments' from various companies of my regiment, with proper officers, stationed in Sandy Hook, Petersville, Jefferson, Urbana, New Market, Buckeyetown, Frederick City and other places where the polls were held. Owing to the presence of the troops everything progressed quietly and I am happy to report a Union victory in every place in my jurisdiction.[2]

Other citizens suspected of being in opposition to the government were required to swear an oath of allegiance before polling. Lord Lyons, the

British minister to the United States, complained of these arrests and wrote to his home government:

> A war has been made at Baltimore [and other places] upon particular articles of dress, particular colors, portraits of Southern leaders and other supposed symptoms of supposed disaffection. The violent measures which have been resorted to have gone far to establish the fact that Maryland is retained in the Union only by military force. They have undoubtedly increased the dislike of the people to their Northern ruler.[3]

Just prior to polling day, Union army volunteers from the state were furloughed and encouraged to cast ballots, as were non-Marylanders in the Northern army. This type of military intimidation and fraud typified the pattern of elections in Maryland throughout the war.[4] It seems strange that so many modern historians have been able to overlook these facts and convince themselves that Maryland, "though on the brink of secession...righted itself" and aligned firmly with the Union.[5] Perhaps the temptation to align themselves with the liberal vogue of the late 20th century is too great.

Augustus W. Bradford, a conservative Unionist and strong supporter of the federal government, was elected governor on November 6, 1861, by a large majority, as was a general assembly of predominantly Unionist members. The States Rights or Southern Rights party, made up of older men unable to serve in the Southern army, could offer no real political threat, hindered as they were by the Northern army. Their nomination for governor of Benjamin Chew Howard, son of a Revolutionary War hero whose sons now served in the Confederate Army, was symbolic of the party's appeal. In the face of Union soldiers voting "everywhere freely without hindrance, and fully without denial, and speedily without delay, and as much and as often as they chose,"[6] the States Rights organization could never be more than a noisy annoyance in the era of the trampled ballot.

With an eye to tying Maryland more firmly to the Union, Governor Hicks immediately called the new Unionist legislature into special session in Annapolis. It convened on December 3, 1861, and rushed to undo all that the preceding Rebel or Confederate legislature had done in support of the South and in opposition to the federal government. It was now resolved that the state was devoted to the Union and had confidence in Lincoln, while denouncing a speech by Jefferson Davis in which he declared, "Maryland already united to us by hallowed ties and material interests, will when able to speak with an unstifled voice, unite her destiny with the South."[7]

The new legislature passed a treason law calling for the death penalty to anyone convicted of levying war against the state, or to anyone giving aid to such persons. The resolutions acquitting Baltimore authorities of blame for the events of April 19th were repealed and replaced by a $7,000 appropriation for the families of the Sixth Massachusetts, but nothing for the families of those citizens slain by the troops. The legislators agreed that Maryland's quota of troops would be financed by a direct tax called for by the United States government, yet adamantly stated that the war was being supported to restore the Union only, and in no way was the institution of slavery to be altered.[8] Except for the gallant but meager attempts at opposition from the older Democrats, the official organs of Maryland's political life had passed completely into the hands of the federal administration.

As the opposing armies struggled across Maryland and Virginia, the iron grip of the vast federal war machine, which deployed 250,000 men in the Chesapeake region,[9] kept the state under control but could not keep the Unionist party from splitting on the Negro question.

The Unionist party from 1861 to 1865 was really the product of Maryland's unsuccessful struggle to resist Northern coercion and the state's subsequent occupation. With the aid of the federal army, those Unionists still loyal to Lincoln in spite of his policies were able to dominate local and statewide elections in 1861 and 1862. The new "party of loyalty's" sweeping victory was marred by the efforts of military officials to insure a crushing Union majority. In spite of fraudulent voting practices by federal soldiers, voter turnout was barely kept above half the normal level.[10]

The victorious Unionists of 1861 and 1862 busied themselves by suppressing the Democrats, solidifying their newly won positions, and obeying the federal administration's demands to prosecute the war effort. Though voting together in denying Congress the right to interfere with the institutions of any state and condemning that body's emancipation of slaves in the District of Columbia, Maryland Unionists could not agree on the future of slavery and of free Negroes. The reaction to federal policies concerning the institution of slavery in the states created a split in the party that would ultimately result in the destruction of the Unionist organization in Maryland.

During the early stages of the war, the Lincoln administration took care not to anger the border states by disrupting the institution of slavery in the occupied areas. In Maryland, the federal army threatened its soldiers with military and civil punishment if caught inciting slave insubordination and even offered to aid in the suppression of rumored servile insurrections.[11] Furthermore, strict military regulations were set forth regarding the use of colored labor and the return of fugitive slaves to their rightful owners. But repeated warnings could not keep the slaves from slipping within army lines and the Union troopers gladly using them as servants and laborers. Citizen's committees complained that the noncompliance of federal authorities with the Fugitive Slave Law had allowed army camps and the District of Columbia to become a haven for runaways. In response to these complaints Lincoln promised to do something about the problem, but it only intensified. Military officials continued to break the law and indignantly threaten the lives of legitimate owners who protested.[12]

With the war going badly for the North in 1862, Lincoln changed his policy on slavery for political and military reasons. The president pushed an act through Congress which called for compensated emancipation in the District of Columbia and urged that a similar resolution be passed for the border states. This was an attempt by Lincoln to destroy the bonds between border slave states and the Confederacy, thereby crushing any hopes that the two could unite. This political ploy outraged Union men in Maryland, many of whom, including newly-elected Governor Bradford, were still slaveholders. They argued that it was political suicide for loyal Unionists to be aligned with the administration's abolitionist policies and unfair to Maryland's economic and social interests—not to mention the state's Negroes, who would be cast adrift in a system where they would struggle to compete.[13]

Lincoln hoped for a Union victory on the battlefield in 1862, so that he could issue his preliminary Emancipation Proclamation. The bloody standoff at Sharpsburg and Lee's withdrawal back across the Potomac would have to suffice. The president's proclamation, technically not intended as a blow to slavery but to the Confederacy's power to conduct foreign policy and make war,[14] further exacerbated the problems of Maryland's Union party and its slaveholders.[15] Amid Northern and border state protests against the proclamation and subsequent Republican reverses in the congressional elections of 1862, Lincoln tried to "take the sting out of the issue." He proposed voluntary compensated emancipation up through the year 1900, as well as further talk of colonization schemes. These proposals quieted the uproar but were never acted upon, and on

January 1, 1863, the document became law.

Paragraph nine of the proclamation allowed for free Negroes to be "received into the armed service of the United States to garrison forts, positions, stations, and other places, and to man vessels of all sorts in said service."[16] By the summer of 1863, overzealous Union recruiting officers, such as Colonel Creager in Western Maryland and Colonel Birney on the Eastern Shore, were enticing slaves to enlist literally by the boatload. Marylanders had a just right to complain for several reasons. The illegal rounding up of able-bodied male slaves deprived the state of needed labor now that most of her white men were at war and left the slaveowners with the added burden of looking after the women, children and older Negroes. This exacerbated the problems Maryland had in fulfilling its federal quota for troops.

The delegates at the constitutional convention, though praising the use of Negro troops to free white soldiers for combat, complained that the slaves from Maryland should be counted toward the state's quota, not to fill the quotas of officers from New York and New Jersey who set up recruiting stations and enticed the slaves with newly printed greenbacks.[17]

Even Unionists considered to be loyal were not allowed to challenge military authority. In one instance, Colonel Sothoren, a planter from St. Mary's County, was told by a Union officer in charge of a group of Negro soldiers that he had come to carry off his able-bodied slaves. Sothoren informed the officer that he was welcome to all who chose to accompany him, at which time the colonel's slaves all declined to leave. The officer stated his determination to carry them off anyway, and the planter expressed his determination to protect his people. A struggle ensued, and Colonel Sothoren killed the officer, wounded a Negro soldier, and later evaded federal vengeance by escaping to Virginia for the remainder of the war.[18]

Masters attempting to identify their fugitive slaves for future compensation were bullied, and threats of retaliation abounded on both sides. Slaveowners and conservative Unionists, led by Governor Bradford, complained vehemently but to little avail. Secretary of War Edwin M. Stanton "regarded the enlistment of slaves in Maryland as a military necessity which would allow the release of white soldiers for other duties," but by September promised that in the future only "disloyal" slaveowners would not be compensated for losses.[19]

Some owners who took the oath of allegiance and manumitted their slaves to the army received compensation, not to exceed $300 per enlistee, which was but a fraction of pre-war values. But according to United States senator from Maryland, Reverdy Johnson, the army persisted in its illegal actions. Union officers in steamboats would travel down the long rivers of the state enlisting slaves at night by merely telling them that they must join the army.[20] The entire issue became meaningless on October 13, 1864, when slavery was abolished in Maryland by ratification of the state's new constitution.[21] Members of the Unionist party in Maryland resisted debate on the divisive issue of slavery until it was forced on them by Lincoln's use of the Negro against the South. One has to wonder how many of Maryland's so-called Unionists who had not already broken ranks due to Lincoln's coercive policies would have gladly joined the Democrats or their statesmen to the south in fighting for the Confederacy had not the Union army been there to stop them.

Many prominent Unionists, including those from the western counties, believed that free Negroes were a "curse to the State," and that any party affiliated with the abolitionist movement was doomed to failure in Maryland.[22] These members of the legislature thought Maryland already had too many free Negroes. Since the "North would not have them," and hardly anyone believed in the sincerity of Lincoln's plans to colonize them in Africa, they asked where these freed slaves were to go.[23] The Conservative Unionists, as they came to be called, did not want race to become a factor in Maryland politics and called on the president to wage war for the restoration of the Constitution and Union only. They ridiculed Lincoln's emancipation policies as playing into the hands of the Democrats by undermining the government's white power base.[24] The Conservative Unionists were opposed by the "unconditional men" or radicals in their party, so named for their unconditional support of Lincoln's administration and their radical ideas favoring the emancipation of Maryland's slaves.

The Conservatives were what remained of the Union State Central Committee following the defection of the radicals and their subsequent formation of the Grand Union League in the spring of 1863. At first the Conservatives were bullied and overshadowed by the fervent and highly organized radical or unconditional men. But by the fall of 1863, the state central committee, led by prominent Unionists such as Governor Bradford and Montgomery Blair, was able to control its own nominating conventions and oppose the radicals on most national and statewide tickets. The Conservatives believed in undivided, but not unconditional, support of Lincoln's government. They opposed having Negroes in the army and held that the war was fought for Constitution and Union, not for side issues such as slavery.[25] Conservatives accused their opponents of being abolitionists in favor of Negro equality, Black Republicans, and of being politically self-destructive.[26] The radicals were condemned for their "toadying" up to Lincoln and their greed for wealth and power in doing "the work of prisoners on duty for the cause of abolitionism."[27]

Behind outspoken conservatives like Governor Bradford, whose son was a Confederate officer, and Montgomery Blair, who was postmaster general in Lincoln's cabinet, the state central committee was able to mount a successful campaign based on opposition to radical support of abolition. Bradford argued that support of emancipation policies would prolong the rebellion "by uniting and concentrating its various elements and even bringing to its support many who had hitherto held aloof from it."[28] Blair did not believe that the races could co-exist in peace and continued to urge the federal government to implement its plans for colonization. Knowing that ultra-abolitionist policies would rupture the party and return the Democrats to power, Blair stated that Maryland was "white men's country" and attacked the radical Unionists for trying to create "a hybrid race" by the "amalgamation" of the black element.[29]

The radicals were led by Henry Winter Davis, a complex man and a seemingly confused former Whig, whose overriding political characteristic was his loathing of the Democrats. He opposed Lincoln's harsh war policies and the Emancipation Proclamation but, guided by partisan politics, campaigned for the freeing of Maryland's slaves.[30] Conservative Unionists called him a "paltry coward," "demagogue," "traitor," and "a white Negro."[31] These attacks on Davis and the abolitionist stance of his party proved to be extremely effective and so damaging as to elicit a desperate response from the unconditionals. They called their opponents "rebel sympathizers," "copperheads" and Democrats, and concerning their own implied support of amalgamation between the black and white races, retorted, "The vierest fool in a lunatic asylum knows the two will not be placed on an equality by emancipation."[32]

Despite attempts to mask the open break, by the autumn of 1863 the Unionist party had split into two distinct and opposing factions. In the months preceding the November election, conservative Unionists and Democrats had expressed concern over possible military intervention in favor of the unconditional faction at the polls. Repressive activities, such as the arrest of circuit judge Richard Carmichael, who was beaten with revolver butts and dragged from his courtroom in Easton by federal soldiers for daring to investigate arrests made during the elections of 1861; the forcing of churches and public buildings to fly the Stars and Stripes; the

suppression of certain
newspapers; the banning of the
initials CSA from obituaries
announcing the deaths of
Maryland Confederates; and the
continued arrest and illegal
detention of suspected Southern-
sympathizers on the flimsiest of
evidence, all exhibited the
willingness of the federal
government to use force to insure
the doubtful allegiance of
Maryland.[33]

Some regions of the state, such
as Southern Maryland and the
Eastern Shore, managed to resist
federal occupation better than

USMHI
General Robert E. Schenck

others and could never be brought to heal. In some instances armed groups
of citizens even drove soldiers away from the polls.[34] The fifth election
district, known as "Little Egypt" and comprising Prince Georges, Charles,
Calvert, St. Mary's, Anne Arundel, Montgomery, Howard and part of
Baltimore counties, elected pro-Confederacy Democrats throughout the
war.[35] Obviously concerned over the split in the Unionist party and the
effect it would have on the state elections in November 1863, the federal
army began to take steps in the hope of insuring a statewide radical victory.

The military commander in Maryland, General Robert E. Schenck,
issued his General Orders No. 53, which called for Union troops to once
again patrol the polls and ordered the arrest of all "disloyal persons" who
were guilty of "hanging about or approaching any poll or place of election."
The order also instructed provost marshals to "assist" election judges in
administering the oath of allegiance and to report any judge who refused
to cooperate.[36] Governor Bradford tried to issue his own proclamation
informing the judges to disregard Schenck's order and assuring them of
protection under state authority, but the general prohibited newspapers
to print the proclamation or to transmit it over the telegraph wires.

In response to continued complaints and seeking to head off a
confrontation, Lincoln intervened. He did not believe "that to keep the
peace at the polls, and to prevent the persistently disloyal from voting,
constitute[d] just cause of offense to Maryland," and reminded Bradford
of the army support that he himself had benefited from during the election

of 1861.[37] The president modified Schenck's order somewhat, though not altering its intent. Bradford's proclamation was eventually allowed to be sent out, but not without an accompanying copy of the president's letter of rebuttal.[38]

Neither opposition complaints nor Lincoln's soothing words could prevent direct and open army interference in favor of the radicals during the election of 1863. As in earlier elections, arrests were made and ballots were disallowed. In some instances politically ambitious Union officers, by this time running for office on the unconditional ticket, even had conservative members of their own party arrested.[39] The result was a landslide victory for the radical faction in what was, considering the circumstances, a light voter turnout. The party of emancipation now controlled twelve of the twenty-one seats in the Senate, fifty-two out of seventy-four seats in the House, four out of five United States congressional seats, and won the important race for state comptroller.[40]

The new unconditional legislature met for the first time in January of 1864 and wasted no time in taking advantage of its control of both houses. Amid tense debate, a bill was passed in February which called for a referendum on the need to call a constitutional convention. To expedite matters, the legislation called for delegates to the proposed convention to be elected at the same time. There was also a stipulation requiring that voters in the referendum take the new "iron-clad loyalty oath."[41]

Sensing the futility of further opposition to the radicals on the emancipation issue, some Conservative Unionists, motivated by a sense of political expediency, began to compromise in hope of maintaining some control in their party. Montgomery Blair had foreseen the growing power of the federally backed unconditionals and earlier had written, "We can only succeed in defeating the abolitionists by [politically clearing ourselves of pro-slavery sentiments] and by forcing them to come to the real issue which involves the relations of the freed Negroes to the whites."[42] The referendum held in April differed little from the previous election concerning army interference, with the radicals winning by a three to two majority. Southern Maryland and only four counties on the Eastern Shore were able to resist the obvious move toward abolition.[43]

The delegates hastened to Annapolis, where they began the lengthy debates that would last until September. The unconditional Unionists controlled the proceedings and from the beginning took steps designed to solidify their dominance and ensure its longevity. In a move designed to strengthen the Union party in Maryland, representation was reapportioned by legislation, which changed the system from one based on total population to one based on white population only. This would increase the number of delegates from Baltimore and the western counties, while decreasing the number from areas of high slave concentration. The radicals continued to press for ways of inequitably reducing the number of assemblymen from the rural counties, but the debate halted abruptly when Democrats pointed out that if the slaves were truly to be emancipated, then representation must revert back to total population.[44] As one Democratic leader sarcastically pointed out, the abolitionists were great friends of the Negro "up to a certain point."[45]

These political wranglings were intensified by a number of occurrences during the summer of 1864. Newspaper reports of racial mixing in the state played on the hatred of the free Negroes in Maryland and inspired delegates to denounce any steps that would lead to "intermarriage and commingling of the races."[46] Conservatives continued to vote with the Democrats on issues concerning free Negroes and slaves, but the emancipation clause eventually passed 53 to 27 by a strict Union party vote. Jubal Early's Confederate raid on the Union capital raised a storm of indignation from the unconditionals who retaliated by passing yet another set of restrictive resolutions. They demanded that the federal government imprison or banish all citizens who persisted in open sympathy with the South, had aided or even "expressed sympathy with" Early's Confederates, or who had refused to sign a new loyalty oath.[47]

These petty resolutions were followed by a more practical one that sought to guarantee Unionist hegemony for some time to come. A provision was included in the new constitution requiring voters to take yet another new and improved "iron-clad oath," which demanded that citizens now swear "past and future loyalty" to the Union. This astute move created two great, and what appeared to be lasting, advantages for the radicals. They would be able to "forever" disenfranchise Democrats who could not take the oath, including Confederate veterans upon their return home after the war and, by having the new oath provision applied to the upcoming referendum, would ensure ratification of their partisan and unconditional constitution.[48]

The results of the referendum held in October must have filled the radicals with alarm and been an inspiration to the Democrats. The citizens of Maryland rejected the new constitution by a two-thousand-vote majority, but the soldiers in the federal army who cast 2,633 votes in favor and 263 against the constitution, ratified it by 375 votes. Thus, in an election where a large percentage of voters were either out of the state or disenfranchised and the remainder influenced by an occupation army, the basic set of laws by which Marylanders would henceforth run their society was in many ways diametrically changed by the votes of 375 soldiers, assuming, of course, that the poll was fairly counted in the first place.

The outcome of the referendum, and of the national and statewide elections a few weeks later in November, highlighted the fractious condition of the Union party and the declining fortunes of the radicals. The seat of arch-radical leader Henry Winter Davis was

Maryland State Archives
Thomas Swann

taken by a conservative, and Democrats from the Eastern Shore and Southern Maryland won seats in the United States Congress. Thomas Swann, the conservative-sponsored nominee of the Unionist party, won election as Maryland's new governor, thereby insuring powerful influence for his faction in the future. Of the less than 70,000 votes reported, Lincoln received only fifty-two percent, despite army interference, a strictly enforced test oath and a suspect provision which allowed soldiers in units serving outside of the state to have their votes collected and cast by officers.[50]

General George B. McClellan, veteran of many clashes with Lee and commander at the great battle of Sharpsburg, Maryland, was the Democratic candidate for president in 1864, and ran on a platform calling for an end to the war and the recognition of the Confederacy. He was unpopular with Maryland Democrats for his role in the occupation of the state during the first years of the war, but in what must have been a combination of yet-eligible Democrats and disgruntled conservative Unionists, the general managed to control large sections of the state. McClellan received eighty-six percent and sixty-four percent of the vote from Southern Maryland and the Eastern Shore respectively, as well as high percentages in most of the northern and western counties, but could not overcome the administration's advantages in Maryland. By strict application of the test oath in populous, federally controlled areas such as Baltimore, where Lincoln received eighty-three percent of the vote, the president was able to eke out a victory over his Democratic opponent.[51]

With its most energetic element either fighting for the Confederacy or languishing in federal prisons and the state occupied by the army of an arch-rival Republican, it would seem surprising that the Democratic party could have remained a viable force in Maryland politics. A lack of cohesion from the national party organization, trampled ballots, hatred of test oaths and disenfranchisement all contributed to the dismal showings of the Democrats in statewide elections during the first few years of the war. Knowing the kind of interference the label "Democrat" would elicit from federal forces, the organization even began to conduct campaigns under various titles such as the States Rights or Southern Rights party.

But by utilizing cells of loyal support and friendly newspapers and, most of all, by dominating local elections in the rural areas, the Democrats were able to maintain their party organization. By controlling county governments, long a strong force in Maryland politics, the Democrats were able to fill one third of the seats in the legislature throughout the war. This retrenching and concentrating on local elections, less easily trampled by federal authorities, enabled the Democratic party to survive and Marylanders to maintain control of their slaves and localities. When the opportunity to reestablish the party as a statewide force presented itself in 1864, the Democrats and the people of Maryland were ready.

Encouraged by the split in the Unionist organization, and roused to action by the attempt of that party to rewrite Maryland's constitution, the Democrats sprang into action during 1864 to revitalize their statewide election apparatus. Though soundly defeated in the April referendum, the Democrats worked hard during the constitutional debates to resist the Unionist machinations. Though hatred of free Negroes was non-partisan in Maryland, the Democrats were able to damage the Unionist image by labeling that party's attempt to re-write the constitution as a support of race-mixing. Democratic journals extolled the need for a "white man's party formed on the single issue of opposition to abolition. Too long already has the Negro been pushed forward and the white man thrust back."[52]

The Democrats denounced the opposition's attempts to emancipate Maryland's slaves, declare the United States government supreme over the state government and pass resolutions designed to disenfranchise "disloyal" citizens.[53] In a tried and true grass roots campaign, Democratic members of the legislature travelled extensively across the state, speaking out against radical-sponsored initiatives. They also had copies of their fiery constitutional debate speeches printed up and distributed. Considering the extenuating circumstances surrounding the election and the small margin by which the constitution was passed, the Democrats must have been very successful in resurrecting party support and in convincing conservative Unionists to vote across party lines.

Leading this resurgence were old-time Democrats such as state chairman Oden Bowie, a member of an influential Prince Georges County family. He ran the family's extensive holdings during the war when his sons, brothers and nephews served in the Confederate army. Utilizing effective slogans such as "Constitution as it is, Union as it was, and a white man's party," and "Constitution as it is, Union as it was, and Negroes where they were," the state organization was almost able to deliver Maryland's electoral votes to the Democrats in November of 1864, even with local resistance to McClellan. This revitalization of the Democrats, soon to be greatly enhanced by returning Confederates at the end of hostilities in the spring of 1865, made the Unionist factions scramble for ways of maintaining political control in Maryland.

Lacking a cohesive bond with the radicals now that the war would not be an issue, the conservative Unionists, whose party had a short time before called Democrats "the party of Dixie, Davis, and the Devil,"[54] began to seek an alliance with their former opponents. Despite the similarity of views on some issues, the Democrats refused to follow along in league with the conservative Unionists and their policy of appeasement.[55] The radicals took a different tack altogether. Instead of trying to work with either the conservatives in their own party or the Democrats, they used what was left of their control in the legislature to pass a registry bill designed to disenfranchise any opposition. Conservative Unionists and Democrats alike vehemently opposed this bill, calling it an attempt by "political cliques straining every nerve to perpetuate their powers,"[56] and a design to "force their doctrines of Negro equality upon the country."[57] The political struggle for control of Maryland would be more evenly matched and fought during the era of Reconstruction.

Notwithstanding the Democratic and conservative victories, the radicals were still in control of the assembly when it convened in January of 1865. They hurriedly implemented the new constitution, ratified the Thirteenth Amendment and destroyed a substantial part of Maryland's slave code, but the most controversial piece of partisan legislation passed was the Registration Act. The other bills could eventually be overturned by a new legislature, but not if, by the use of a restrictive registration law, the radicals insured that in the future only their adherents were eligible to vote.

Thomas Swann, Maryland's new conservative governor, a one-time staunch Unionist, now began to look past party affiliations and mold his policies in response to the fast changing Reconstruction atmosphere. Though not pressing for an immediate reversal of radical initiatives, Swann endorsed President Andrew Johnson's liberal treatment of the defeated Southern states, and held that the treatment of the South must be decided by the "Anglo-Saxon race."[58] He opposed Negro suffrage and the absurd "threats held out by some, that no state should resume her former status in the Union, without a transfer of the political power which she had always exercised, to the control of the Negro race."[59]

The breach within the Unionist organization continued to expand as Maryland conservatives backed the president and the radicals supported Congress in the national struggle over Reconstruction. In Maryland, like the rest of the South, the Reconstruction battle hinged on two important political problems: the fight over the Registration Act (or the disenfranchisement of Confederate veterans and Democrats) and Negro suffrage. The conservatives, led by Governor Swann and the prominent Unionist Montgomery Blair, sided with the Democrats in opposition to the radicals, who wished to exclude all but themselves and their Negro allies from voting. Blair accelerated the attack on Congress and the radicals by accusing them of using "the African race" to maintain power and further incited white Marylanders by stating, "The hired beagle of the Civil Rights bill will hunt the white man down at his home or drive him from it."[60]

The issue of what was to become of free Negroes intensified during the summer of 1866, as conservatives rushed to follow Blair's lead in condemning radical supported race-mixing. A Frederick newspaper had this to say:

> Rampant fanatical abolitionism gloated with its success, drunk with bloodraving and with its insane heresies is pressing furiously onward to its legitimate consequence—the goal of full social equality for the Negro with all the degrading horrors of amalgamation. Be not deceived: our very firesides are threatened and unless men act and act with vigor, even race itself as well as home will be prostituted to the orgies of this great Moloch of America.[61]

The radicals responded to these damaging attacks by "waving the bloody shirt" and making a futile attempt to disassociate themselves from the Negro suffrage movement. They pleaded with Union sympathizers to exclude from power men "who with Gilmor and Johnson sought to raze our [state and] now want power back."[62] Somehow the Radicals attempted to justify their support of the Fourteenth Amendment, which made Negroes citizens, while at the same time denying their support of Negro suffrage "at this time, in any manner, and any and everywhere."[63] The final break came during the autumn of 1866, when Governor Swann fulfilled his promise that the Registration Act would not be "made the instrument of degradation of our people in the hands of vindictive and radical agents."[64]

In the Baltimore municipal elections of October, the unconditional faction employed such vindictive agents to their benefit. A partisan decision by attorney general Alexander Randall allowed the radicals to apply the registration list of 1865 and thereby disenfranchise Democrats and many conservatives. The radicals easily re-elected their mayor and dominated the city council. They would also certainly control the city's eighteen pivotal seats in the House of Delegates unless something was done before the upcoming November election. Swann, who had already enraged the unconditionals by using his powers under the Registration Act to appoint only conservative and Democratic registrars statewide, was determined to wrest control of Baltimore away from the radical machine.

The governor began by ordering the radical police commissioners, who were in charge of Baltimore's partisan election officials, to stand trial before him on charges of "official misconduct."[65] He found the commissioners guilty and replaced them with two men of his own who had instructions to appoint impartial election judges. The radicals responded in their usual way by threatening armed resistance and having their man, judge Hugh Lennox Bond, issue warrants for the arrest of the governor's new appointees on charges of conspiracy. Unwilling to bow to such illegal actions, Swann discussed the problem with his ally, President Johnson, who pledged to insure order and fair play by using regular United States military if need be. Even though the unconditional election judges remained in place and the party resorted to old tricks like coloring ballot tickets, it could not prevent all of the Democrats from voting. Under the watchful eyes of a regiment sent by the president, the Democrat/conservative coalition swept all eighteen seats in Baltimore and sixty out of eighty statewide.[66] The November elections resulted in the collapse of the Union party movement not only in Maryland but also nationwide. In Maryland, the conservatives, long anxious to employ Democrats in a coalition under their hegemony, now were forced into the stronger camp of their allies. The vastly outnumbered radicals limped into the camp of the Republicans and resorted to begging Congress for intervention on their behalf. The stage was now set for the rejuvenated Democratic party to undo radical legislation and solidify its control of the state.

In January of 1867 the new legislature ardently endorsed the governor's call for new municipal elections in Baltimore and the summoning of a new constitutional convention. The representatives also sided with Swann in support of President Johnson's Reconstruction policy and opposed the Fourteenth Amendment.[67] The constitution of 1864 had been forced on Maryland at the point of federal bayonets, and many citizens felt that the state's resurgence required the re-writing of that important document.[68] The radicals correctly viewed the writing of a new constitution as a lethal threat to what was left of their political power. Once more they tried to play their old trump card, federal intervention, but were unsuccessful. Their cries that the House of Delegates was full of illegally elected rebels acting outside of state law were treated with contempt and the referendum carried by a staggering majority.[69]

The new constitution called for white male suffrage only, which required but a simple oath of allegiance to the new Union for office-holders and voters alike. In moves designed to strengthen Democratic control, the delegates provided that representation in the Maryland House be based on total black and white population, and increased the conservative element's representation in the Senate by creating a new Eastern Shore county. Somerset and Worcester counties each provided land, and Wicomico County was born. They also called for new municipal elections in Baltimore, now that the city was freed from the fraudulent activities of the radicals. Responding to old Democratic entreaties that the "ballot box" was the only protection "for your altars, your firesides, and your homes,"[70] Maryland voters overwhelmingly approved the new constitution on September 18, 1867, by a two to one majority.[71]

Reeling from one defeat to another, the radical Unionists felt compelled to cast away principles and institute drastic changes. In a panic-stricken attempt to save political fortunes, the Unionist organization changed its name to the Republican Union party and flip-flopped on the race issue by embracing Negro suffrage. These moves were obviously an attempt to gain United States congressional support in arresting by force the Democratic resurgence.

Men such as Hugh Lennox Bond and Senator John Creswell were the leading figures in this newest radical counteroffensive. Bond was an influential Republican judge and fanatical social worker who travelled across the state with a band of Freedman's Bureau officials urging Negroes not to "lay down on the shovel and hoe and subsist upon the mere empty title of freedmen...[but to] eschew intoxicating drinks, avoid thieving, [and] get homes for yourselves."[72] Creswell, Bond's opponent for Republican party control, was critical of the judge for his premature agitation on the race issue and sought to control a smaller, but stronger party based on federal patronage.[73] The vast majority of white Marylanders were understandably adverse to these policies and tactics. Even avowed Republicans in the northern and western counties resisted Negro participation in the politics of the party.[74]

Democratic attacks on Republican support of Negro suffrage were devastating. Even in the mountainous counties which were not conducive to slave labor and had few Negroes, the people strongly embraced Democratic appeals on race. One Allegheny County convention wholeheartedly resolved that "this government was made on the white basis by white men for the benefit of white men."[75] The results of the November election were proof of the innate power behind the appeals used by Republican opponents. The Democratic party was victorious statewide, electing a new mayor of Baltimore and Oden Bowie as governor by a landslide—63,694 to 22,050—over the Republican candidate Hugh Bond.

The Reconstruction struggle officially ended in Maryland with the ratification of the Fifteenth Amendment to the Constitution. Despite federal acts designed to guarantee their equality, Negroes continued to be controlled by whites. Democrats were able to regain and hold control of Maryland through the ballot box, which enabled white citizens to circumvent federal policies and maintain direction of their society. In acts ranging from a state imposed peonage system, where newly freed Negroes convicted of crimes were sold by the courts to farmers for varying periods of time, to an apprenticeship system where contracts on young Negroes were sold to manufacturers, miners, and merchants,[76] whites in Maryland, like the rest of the South, were able to control the Negro population.

Chapter 5

Establishing Maryland's Place in History

To philosopher-historian Oswald Spengler (1880-1936), the American Civil War or War for Southern Independence was just one act in a great drama being played out within western culture as a whole. The Idealistic Spirit, borne for centuries by an hereditary and landed aristocracy, clung desperately to the past against the onslaught of Philosophical Materialism, in which money replaces blood as political power, science drives out religion and the farmer becomes the proletariat and sets the stage for the new values: Internationalism, Egalitarianism, Individualism and Consumerism. To Spengler, this organic aging process played itself out during the epoch from the Age of Enlightenment to the First World War, with the Jacobins of France, the abolitionists of America and the socialists of Germany as the standard bearers for the new age, which he declares as the final stage of a culture and characterizes as "Civilization."

However one cares to view history, as the inevitable unfolding of a destiny or as the meaningless and random flux of cause and effect, the state of Maryland at the midway point of the nineteenth century was at the center of a great cataclysm in human history and experienced its full force and intensity. In the great clash, the people of Maryland, so far as one may generalize, chose clearly to side with the traditional idealistic spirit and its standard bearer, the Confederate States of America.

As in all political controversies, there was never a unanimous feeling in any region of the country concerning the crisis of 1860. Certainly not all Southerners favored secession, nor were all Northerners for coercion. The overriding cause for what anti-secession feeling and hesitancy existed in the South, especially the border slave states, was an unwillingness to see the Union torn asunder. It must be remembered that the Union in 1860 was not that old. The republic was a great and so far successful experiment, something that was not taken for granted in the minds of Americans. Bringing the North American continent under the control of a united English-speaking people was arguably one of the greatest events in the history of the western world. The young country was bound together by the feelings of perceived victory in all its wars, its sense of potential and the lure of westward expansion, and the ever-present danger from jealous European monarchies. The Union, paid for with the blood of their fathers, was to be preserved at all costs. Men waited until the last possible moment before they carelessly tossed away one of the most important aspects of their lives.

Maryland exhibited all the qualities of a Southern state, even more so than Virginia at times. She had taken up every Southern cause since the founding of the nation. She had supported South Carolina in the nullification controversy, repeatedly expressed her hatred of Northern abolitionists, shown an indisputable hatred of the free Negro population, was adamantly in favor of states rights, and had supported the Democrats in 1860, when other great Southern states like Virginia and Tennessee had failed to do so. More importantly, Maryland had rejected Lincoln and the abolitionist stance of the Republican party and instead had cast all of her electoral votes for the Southern Democrats and heavily supported the pro-slavery Constitutional Unionists.

But geography and other uncontrollable factors withheld from Maryland the time to make decisions at her leisure. The old men, the politicians and others with something to lose were against revolutionary change. They made their careers out of the law, respected it, and believed in and honored agreements, unlike many in the North who ignored the law and hurried to subjugate other states, breaking every agreement under the Constitution as fast as their troops could roll into the South by train. The spring of 1861 doomed Maryland to shackles. Practically, she could not secede unless Virginia did so, and by the time her Tidewater partner acted, it was too late.

Governor Thomas Hicks, unquestionably traitorous in his actions toward the citizens of Maryland, and those Unionists as yet unaware of Lincoln's true intentions argued that the best way to protect the institution of slavery in the state was to stay in the Union, where slavery was protected by the Constitution. They were either coldly calculating politicians or suffering from a serious lack of common sense. Could anyone really have believed that the victorious Republicans of 1860 would allow any state, deep south or border, to keep slavery at the end of a bloody war? The Constitution of the United States was interpreted to serve those in power. It is glaringly obvious, and both sides later freely admitted it, that Lincoln and the Republicans of the late nineteenth century manipulated our most respected document in an attempt to legitimize their actions. The abolitionist core in the North, which precipitated the war by operating outside of the law, then carried on a war of conquest, subjugated an entire region of a free country, and has dictated to the people of that region how they should run their society ever since. No matter what personal stance one may choose to take, these facts are inescapable.

With so much material available that points to Maryland being mostly Southern in sympathy, it is amazing that modern writers can conclude that though the state's legislature, newspapers, public meetings, military companies, businesses, plantation owners, and people in the street were staunch Southern sympathizers beyond the point of violence, they righted themselves squarely on the side of the Union in late April of 1861. These authors contradict themselves within their own works. In short quick bursts they admit that the federal army prohibited Maryland from seceding and that the state was in sympathy with the rest of the South before, during, and after the war. However, they then labor to discount the presence of the federal army from late April of 1861 as inconvenient but inconsequential. Of course, Union sentiment exhibited itself from 1861 to 1865—if a Marylander refused to show Union leanings, he was likely to be arrested. A quarter of a million Northern troops guaranteed that.

Some other authors dance around the main issues, seemingly wanting to tell the truth but not wanting to be controversial. Radcliffe states that the vast majority, if not all Marylanders, were against coercion of the Southern states and in opposition to the aims and principles of the Republican party. He also clearly makes the point that even after the Northern invasion, the majority believed the state would eventually join the Confederacy. His book exposes Hicks for what he was in clear terms, at length; and yet, a page later, he expresses puzzlement concerning the mixed signals that the governor was giving. Former governor Enoch Lowe of Maryland has no trouble in defining the vast majority's feelings toward Hicks, calling him

> an unscrupulous hypocrite and infamous two-faced politician of the war variety, [who] had purposely left her [Maryland] in a defenseless position in order that he might without peril to himself deliver her up at the suitable time to be crucified and receive his thirty pieces of silver as the price of his unspeakable treachery.[1]

Hicks allayed the fears of honest people with just the right amount of "what they needed to hear." His treachery bought time, time to sell his own people away. The price was his own material and egotistical enrichment. As with all turncoats throughout history, he was rewarded and then scorned by those whom he betrayed and those with whom he made a devil's pact.

If the political and social statements made by Maryland's citizenry and elected officials prior to April of 1861 were not enough proof of the state's Southern sympathy, then her use of force in resisting the Northern invasion should be. Spilling the first blood of the war in the Baltimore riot, the formation of military companies and attendant monetary actions, and the burning of the bridges and cutting of telegraph wires to the North were conclusive actions for a state which in modern times has been called undecided or Unionist during that era. William Evitts writes that "without question the decision to send troops through Annapolis prevented Maryland from seceding" and labors to prove that Maryland sided with the Union, yet he cannot make the statement without adding that the federal army was very coercive. Authors of the period like J. Thomas Scharf, Mathew P. Andrews, William Glenn, Bradley Johnson, Josiah Benton, W.W. Goldsborough and others leave no doubt that Maryland was Southern in sympathy and would have seceded had not the federal army taken control of the state. The state was occupied and controlled in reality as of April 26, 1861, and all events after that date must be viewed in that light of federal strength and Maryland hopelessness.

Modern authors try to dismiss the pro-Southern events in Maryland prior to the federal takeover as an aberration caused by a small criminal element, when in actuality these events were a mass movement led by the elected representatives and the leading citizens of the state. The small number of determined politicians, like Governor Hicks, were certainly the aberration. When Maryland was firmly in the grasp of Lincoln, Hicks, who had given emotional pro-secession speeches when his life depended on it, was finally unrestrained and celebrated the federal takeover by proclaiming that he would have exonerated Lincoln if he would have hanged "forty of them [secessionist] rascals."[2] Hicks worked hard to assist and press the federals into disarming the local military companies and in stopping supplies and recruits from heading south across the Potomac and from Maryland's Eastern Shore.

As a reward for his treachery, Hicks was appointed brigadier general by Lincoln on July 26, 1862, but never commanded because of ill health. He was then appointed United States senator from Maryland by the new governor on December 27, 1862, to replace the deceased Senator Pearce. Hicks took his seat on January 14, 1863, and went on to have an undistinguished career in the Senate. When addressing that body in an attempt to explain his inconsistent actions over the previous year, Hicks was contradicted and challenged by John Pendleton Kennedy, Maryland's other senator. To this attack, Hicks, who it must be remembered once claimed that he would rather have his right arm torn from his body than to lift it to strike a sister Southern state, retorted that coercion of the seceded states was in his opinion right and that "every rebel, North or South," should be put to death. Hicks did not live long enough to see the war through and after a long illness died on February 13, 1865.

The search for the truth concerning Maryland's feelings in the Civil War era should not stop in April of 1861. The actions of Marylanders during and after the conflict are illuminating. The fantastic contribution by the occupied state of Maryland to the Confederate cause is grossly ignored. The many sizable military units formed from Maryland troops alone, as well as service in the formations from other states, especially those of Virginia, was a unique and tell-tale occurrence. Like the great sacrifices made by the patriots during the Revolutionary War, Maryland's sons fled from their occupied state and fought a war of liberation from outside its borders, against great odds and withstanding extreme hardships.

It is interesting to note that of the 50,000 white Marylanders who were of a military age in 1861 (military service being nowhere near universal in Maryland during that era), 25,000 saw front-line service with the armies and navies of the Confederacy. The Maryland forces who served in the Union armies contained a large percentage of newly arriving immigrants, free Negroes, and forcibly enlisted slaves. Many of these units never saw front-line service, were skeleton formations or were enlisted for short terms near the end of the war.

The Southern-sympathizing Marylanders who were fit for command or of military age left their family, friends and property at the mercy of the invader. Their loved ones were harassed and imprisoned without trial and their property destroyed or confiscated. They risked all to swim across a river and fight in another state's forces, to suffer miserable hardships, sleep outside, eat very little and campaign barefooted. Marylanders who joined the Union did so at their leisure or at the prodding of the federal army, with all the comforts of home, enlistment bonuses in gold, excellent equipment and, in many cases, easy duty at home.

McHenry Howard tells a now humorous story related to the strident efforts of the federal army to recruit in Maryland while he was campaigning with Lee in 1862.

> One day two men came to the house and after parleying with the servant insisted on seeing my mother. They said, "Madam, we are enrolling officers and have come to get the names of male members of your family—have you a husband or sons capable of bearing arms?" She said, "Yes, a husband and six sons." "Your husband, what is his name and where is he?" "Charles Howard, he is a prisoner in Fort Warren." "And your eldest son?" "Frank Key Howard, he is also in prison with his father." "And your next son?" "John Eager Howard, he is a captain in the Confederate Army." "And the next?" "Charles Howard, he is a major in the Confederate Army." "And the next?" "James Howard, he is a lieutenant-colonel in the Confederate Army." "And the next?" "Edward Lloyd Howard, he is a surgeon in the Confederate Army." During this the men had become more and more flustered and faltered out, "And your youngest son?" "McHenry Howard, he is also in the Southern Army and with Stonewall Jackson and I expect he will be here soon." And she shut the door in their faces.[3]

The Southern-sympathizing Marylanders who fought in the field or aided the Confederacy by smuggling men and materials throughout the war risked everything for an idea. They had nothing to gain; they could only lose or maintain the freedoms under the Constitution that their forefathers had given their lives to create and uphold.

Marylanders never hear of these great sacrifices of their forefathers. In this age when the smallest contribution to society is blown out of proportion, it seems sad that in all the history the state's young are required to learn, a great sacrifice like this receives no attention at all. Certainly in Maryland these things should be taught, but why not nationwide for the education of the citizenry? It would give an insight into what politics, government, and the use of force are all about. This lesson could clearly show that the Constitution, for all its good intentions, was manipulated by an activist minority unrepresentative of the will of the people. Maryland was robbed of her freedom of action by the armies of a political party that received less than four out of ten popular votes nationwide.

Lincoln was rejected by the state of Maryland, receiving less than three percent of the popular presidential vote. The Unionist party, which took control of Maryland following the federal occupation, accounted for less than half of the state's electorate in November of 1860. Its numbers decreased steadily as Lincoln carried on his coercive war against the South. Following the Emancipation Proclamation and the subsequent struggle over the future of free Negroes in Maryland, the party then split in half. The ranks of the conservative Unionists or pro-slavery element of the party continued to grow, while the radical or abolitionist faction declined. The radicals fought desperately to maintain their hold on the state. But their use of federal patronage and the Union army to influence elections in Maryland could no longer work in the face of the Democratic/conservative Unionist coalition. Once the Confederate veterans had returned and the conservative Unionists had joined in the Democratic resurgence, the radical faction slipped into the role of a small minority party.

Modern writers or historians have attempted to discount the role played by the federal army and administration in intimidating Maryland voters during the war years. Charles Wagandt and Jean Baker cite many instances of military interference, but then inexplicably dismiss any army intimidation and decrease in voter turnout as inconsequential. They attempt to style the sizable evidence pointing to the phenomenon known as the "Trampled Ballot" as nothing more than the lamentation of defeated Democrats. After the war, the crushing Democratic victories relegated the Republicans in Maryland to a small opposition party crying out for help from their big brothers in the federal government.

What happened to all those Unionist-Republican abolitionists when the Democratic party reasserted itself near the end of the war and into Reconstruction? It would seem apparent that they never existed in large numbers. The wartime success of the anti-Democratic faction in Maryland can be attributed to a relatively small number of highly motivated politicians benefitting greatly from a friendly federal administration and army. Despite Republican dominance of the federal government during the post-war decades, the citizens of Maryland, like those in the rest of the South, regained control of their states by staunchly supporting the Democratic party. Southerners called the Democratic machine "Our Standing Army," and used it to thwart continued Northern attempts to dictate Southern society.

One must but consider two great state symbols, the flag and song, to realize that Confederate sympathy—even better, true *Southernness*— was an actuality in Maryland long after the War Between the States. It is an inescapable fact that "Maryland, My Maryland" is a Confederate battle hymn, one of the most popular, and that it is a rousing call for the state to secede from the Union and fight for the South: "Huzza! she spurns the Northern scum!" The fact that Randall's poem was not made the official state song until 1939 is also very illustrative of Maryland's continued sympathy toward Southern ideals.

The history of Maryland's state flag is equally illuminating. Before the Civil War, Maryland's state flag was simply the banner of the Calvert family, alternating strips of black and gold with vertical interruptions, often emblazoned in the center with the great seal of the Calverts. With their state and her symbols in the hands of federal authorities, the Marylanders who went south to fight for the Confederacy needed a new standard with which to identify. They wanted something that would express their state pride, connect them with Maryland's rich history, exhibit their allegiance to the seceding states, and set them apart from units in the federal army with Maryland designations. The *botonée cross,* or *cross botonée,* was the perfect solution. It was the symbol of Lord Calvert's maternal family, the Crosslands, and could be found on the Great Seal of Maryland from its earliest days. The *cross botonée* was also red and white, the colors of secession, and quite different from the Calvert black and gold that the Union would carry. Maryland Confederates began to wear the cross in the form of a pin attached to the uniform or hat. They also carried the banner into the fray along with the battle flag of the Confederacy. In fact, the *cross botonée* standard of the Second Maryland Infantry, CSA, is reported to be the only state flag carried into the Union lines during Pickett's charge at Gettysburg and then carried out again.

After the war, when Maryland's Confederates took back control of the state, they altered the flag as a mark of their political victory over the Radical Republicans. The first time the flag is seen as it appears today are from pictures taken in 1880 at the celebration of Baltimore City's 150th anniversary. From this point forward, the flag, alternating quarters of the Calvert and Crossland banners, is very prevalent in pictures and tintypes. This banner became the first official state flag of Maryland in 1904.

Even today evidence abounds that Maryland was and in most ways still is a Southern state. It is no mistake that Washington, D.C., was called a sleepy Southern city until the 1960s. Maryland and the District of Columbia had black codes and strictly enforced segregation up until the mid-1950s, while miscegenation was still illegal in Maryland as late as the 1960s. The climate, local dialect, architectural style, and culinary habits are all unmistakably Southern. The Baptist churches of Maryland belong to the Southern Baptist Convention, the University of Maryland is grouped with other Southern universities in the Atlantic Coast Conference, and until recently the Washington Redskins football team proudly displayed the Confederate flag when its marching band played "Dixie" before every home game. I myself attended James Ryde Randall and John Eager Howard Elementary schools, lived around the corner from Roger B. Taney Junior High, and attended Surrattsville Senior High. With the exception of Surrattsville, it was not until I researched Maryland's history as a college student that the significance and Southern nature of those names became evident. These are just some of many examples an observer who spends any time in the area will find.

Great Southern states like Virginia and Tennessee had much larger pro-Union sections than Maryland but were able to secede because of their size and distance from the federal army. In fact, Virginia had an area larger than the entire state of Maryland—West Virginia—break away and become a Northern state, yet it is regarded as one of the greatest of the Southern states.

The states rights question, for all practical purposes, was answered and finalized in blood—or so it seems. Those rights strictly prohibited to the federal government and defined by the Constitution are now binding upon the individual states themselves. The Tenth Amendment is nullified. The federal government now has the power to assert itself without restraint. We are no longer a union of sovereign states but a nation ruled from above. In a society thus united, the realities of force guarantee that the centers of population and wealth must dominate and dictate the future. And now Maryland, a small state dominated by two urban centers, is more and more being drawn into the psychology of the North, and its Southerness is becoming more and more a faint and wistfully lingering ghost.

If the citizens of the United States are to live freely under the ideals of the founding fathers, then the long and continuing trend of domination by the federal government—an occurrence the founding fathers warned against—must end. If the history of the American people is to be anything but a short experiment with freedom, then the true principles of the founding fathers must be reclaimed by the people—not by professional politicians, but by citizens who must reject control and manipulation by ruling cliques to the detriment of the majority. The Tenth Amendment in our Bill of Rights is quite simple and clear on this point: "The powers not delegated to the United States by the Constitution, nor prohibited by it to the States, are reserved to the States respectively, or to the people."

Chapter Six

Marylanders in Battle

Marylanders suffered throughout the war and afterward from politics and legislation that rarely reflected their will. In combat, however, their will was expressed rather clearly. No telling of Maryland's story in the War Between the States would be complete without a military overview of the saga. The major clashes in the decisive theater of operations occurred on Maryland soil or in close proximity in neighboring Virginia and Pennsylvania. Maryland's citizenry, above and beyond the trials of living in a state occupied by what amounted to an occupation army, were directly affected socially, economically, and politically by the presence of half a million armed men locked in a death struggle.

To gain an accurate picture of the strengths and accomplishments of military units during the war one must first know and understand the completely different circumstances under which each side recruited and enlisted Marylanders. For the most part, a young Southern recruit, being drawn to an unknown fate, left his home, his loved ones and his belongings in the uncertain hands of a hostile and sometimes destructive occupying army. These idealistic warriors sacrificed all worldly comforts electing to endure hunger, the elements, poor supply conditions, and death in the unrelenting struggles of a vastly outnumbered army—all this for an ideal gladly suffered. No conquests or great enrichments awaited them if victorious, only the maintenance of the great compact and principles for which their forefathers had fought time and again.

Due to the destruction of official records, it is impossible to determine the exact number of Marylanders who fought for the Confederacy. Estimates range from twenty to thirty thousand. There is evidence that over twenty-one thousand sons of the Old Line State fought in the armies of the South;[1] but one must consider that unknown thousands of

Marylanders were scattered in units from every state in the Confederacy and played a prominent role in its navy. Of those Maryland Confederates lucky enough to evade the mass of Northern militia employed to prevent them going south, it was said they

> embodied the faith and pride of the State. Not a historic family of Maryland but was represented in the Maryland Line. Five grandsons of John Eager Howard, of the Cowpens, carried sword or musket in the First Maryland regiment. A grandson of Charles Carroll of Carrollton rode as a private in Company K, First Virginia cavalry. Colonel Johnson, of the Maryland Line, rode at the head of seventy-two kinsmen, descendants of soldiers of the Revolution, his own flesh and blood![2]

and,

> It is certain that there was no neighborhood in Maryland from Mason and Dixon's line to the seashore, from which all the young men of the better class did not go to military service in Virginia ... [and] a large percentage ... of the officers in the army and navy of the United States from Maryland, resigned their commissions, and entered the service of the Confederacy.[3]

When the facts are considered, it would seem fair to estimate that at least twenty-five thousand, if not thirty thousand, native Marylanders served in the armed forces of the Confederate States of America. As we shall see, these thousands produced men of the highest character and ability. Seventeen went on to attain flag or general rank. In fact, many deserving Marylanders were delayed promotion or did not attain a rank commensurate with their abilities due to the overabundance of leadership material from the state. At one point, Stonewall Jackson's three brigadier generals in the army of the Valley were Marylanders, as were the greatest heroes in the annals of the Confederate navy.[4]

It must also be remembered that the sacrifice and lineage of some of those Marylanders who fought for the Union were no less than that of their Confederate counterparts. The term "brother against brother" took on a literal meaning for some citizens of the Old Line State. There are many recorded instances where brothers, uncles, cousins, sons and fathers from Maryland and the other border states killed or captured each other on bloody fields from the Mississippi to the Atlantic.

Maryland Units in the Federal Army

There were many Maryland units in the Union army by name, but few fully rostered with native Marylanders. Several units were shells only or comprised re-enlisting veterans who joined newly christened regiments upon the expiration of their term of service. Maryland filled only 61% of the quota for troops demanded by the federal government, the lowest of any state technically remaining in the Union. In fact, the large majority of these units were composed of newly arrived foreigners, or, in the case of the numerous Negro regiments with a Maryland designation, were composed of illegally enlisted slaves. Many of these regiments were formed for home defense only, and others near the end of the war were enlisted for periods ranging from 100 days to six months.[5]

In contrast to their Confederate counterparts, the military experience must have been appreciably less demanding for Union volunteers. Union regiments from Maryland serving near home or with the federal military juggernaut were certainly better supplied and paid than most armies anywhere. While the Southern recruit left home with only what he could carry, his Union counterpart received a cash bonus, coerced from the city of Baltimore by threats and a physical assault on the second branch of the city council,[6] and all the martial finery that Governor Hicks and the newly elected legislature could provide.[7] Though never matching the reputation for dash and gallantry achieved by their Southern counterparts, Marylanders in the Northern army nonetheless performed admirable service in picket duty and on battlefields from Manassas to Appomattox.

Fearful of citizen reaction in April of 1861, Governor Hicks balked at Lincoln's call for four regiments of volunteers from the state of Maryland. The federal government then commissioned James Cooper of Frederick to raise a brigade, and recruiting was begun in Baltimore and the western counties. By mid-summer of 1861, the First Regiment, Infantry, Maryland Volunteers, with John R. Kenly as colonel, had been mustered into the service of the United States and guarded the fords of the Potomac. The First fought bravely with General Nathaniel Banks in 1862, as he pursued the army of Stonewall Jackson in the Shenandoah Valley. After its destruction at the hands of the First Maryland Infantry, CSA, at Front Royal, Virginia,[8] it was reorganized in Baltimore and later served with distinction in the Army of the Potomac under various leaders. The unit was credited with taking part in twenty-eight battles and skirmishes and mustered out at Arlington Heights, Virginia, July 2, 1865.[9]

The Second and Third regiments campaigned on the coast of North

Carolina, northern Virginia and eastern Tennessee and distinguished themselves at Sharpsburg in the charge across Burnside's Bridge, at Gettysburg, and later in the final push to Appomattox. The units designated Maryland volunteers, fourth through thirteenth regiments, saw little action. They were primarily used for picket duty and the guarding of prisoners or were six-month and hundred-day units mustered into service near the close of hostilities.[10]

After the recruitment of the First regiment, the subsequent commands designated Maryland volunteers were for the most part composed of foreigners. The Fourth Regiment, for example, was predominantly German. These European immigrants were prevalent throughout the Northern army. New to the country and schooled in the standing armies of the continent, these immigrants gladly used soldiering as a way to stay employed and quickly become part of the mainstream of American society. It was noted that

> these first forces raised for the Union in Maryland were, with the exception of the First regiment, mainly composed of foreigners, aliens by birth and aliens to the institutions, ideals and motives that for nine generations had formed the character of Marylanders. They were good men, but they were not Marylanders. They were devoted to the Union, but they had no conception of the force and duty of "courage and chivalry." The First Maryland under Kenly was the only Maryland regiment on the Union side.[11]

The Potomac Home Brigade, the Purnell Legion and the First and Second Eastern Shore regiments were all Maryland units organized for home defense only. Later in the war, elements of these units participated in the Valley campaigns until surrendering to Jackson at Harpers Ferry. Other elements fought gallantly at Sharpsburg, and later at Gettysburg, where they came face-to-face with the Second Maryland Infantry, CSA, and performed valuable garrison duty on the rail lines vital to the Army of the Potomac.[12]

The First Regiment of Cavalry, Maryland Volunteers, was recruited between August 1861 and June 1862, and consisted of companies from the Baltimore area, Washington and Allegheny counties, Pittsburgh, Pennsylvania, and Washington, D.C. The First became part of the cavalry corps in the Army of the Potomac and was credited with participating in sixty skirmishes and battles during the campaigns in Maryland, Virginia and Pennsylvania before being mustered out of service on August 8, 1865.[13] Maryland also furnished the Union a battalion of artillery consisting of Batteries A & B Maryland Light Artillery. These gunners fought at Malvern Hill, Sharpsburg, Gettysburg, and New Bridge over the Chickahominy, where the unit engaged in an artillery duel with the First Maryland Artillery, CSA, in which both sides sustained considerable damage.[14]

The following list of Marylanders who attained flag or general rank in the Union service requires some explanation. Technically, there were twelve Union general or flag officers from Maryland. However, only six are included herein. There is a good reason for the omissions: merely commanding a unit with a Maryland designation does not a Marylander make. Recent immigrants who received commissions from Maryland, a state whose armed forces were dominated by the federal government, should not be viewed in the same light as officers from old families. Maryland's Confederate generals, by contrast, were all native born with the lone exception of Isaac Trimble. Trimble was a Virginian, the closest of relations, was associated with Maryland from 1832 on, and had even been appointed to command the Volunteer Corps of Baltimore in April of 1861.

The six Union generals not included here had dubious connections with Maryland at best. General Leopold Blumenberg, for instance, was born in Prussia and did not come to Baltimore until 1854. Brigadier General Richard Neville Bowerman came to Maryland during the war as a lieutenant in the New York volunteers. Brigadier General James Cooper was a native of Maryland but spent almost his entire adult life in Pennsylvania, where he served as the state's attorney general and United States senator. In the cases of brigadier generals John Watts Horn and Charles Edward Phelps, both arrived as children in the 1840s, the former from Scotland, the latter from Vermont. The lineage of the last of the omitted six, Brigadier General David Leroy Stanton, is sketchy. Stanton entered the First Maryland Infantry as a sergeant and was only brevetted a brigadier general from April 1, 1865.

Union General and Flag Officers from Maryland

Major General **Andrew Woods Denison** (1831-1877) of Baltimore was a lieutenant in the Baltimore City Guards until that organization disbanded in 1861. He was commissioned in July 1862 as colonel of the Eighth Maryland, and later commanded the Maryland Brigade. Wounded at Laurel Hill during the battle of Spotsylvania in May 1864, he lost his right arm and was promoted brigadier general for meritorious conduct. During the action at White Oak Road in March 1865, he was again severely wounded and later promoted to major general for his gallantry. Following the war he was judge of the appeal tax court, postmaster of Baltimore City, and first commander of the Grand Army of the Republic in Maryland.[15]

 Major General **William Hemsley Emory** (1811-1887) of Queen Anne's County graduated from West Point in 1831 and served at several seaports as an artillery officer. He became interested in topographical engineering and was assigned to duty on the northeast boundary survey and later on the Delaware River project making navigational improvements. During the war with Mexico he served as a staff officer to General Stephen Kearney and was twice commended for his actions. After the war he participated in the survey of the border between Mexico and the United States according to the Gadsden Treaty of 1853. He was promoted to lieutenant colonel of cavalry in May of 1861. He fought in the Peninsular Campaign and attained the rank of brigadier general in March 1862. Emory later commanded a division under General Banks in Louisiana and upon promotion to major general led a corps in the Red River Expedition. Back in Virginia in 1864, he saw action under Sheridan in the Shenandoah Valley at Opequon Creek, Fisher's Hill, and Cedar Creek. General Emory was five times commended for his actions during the conflict and following the war was given command of several military departments.[16]

Major General **William Henry French** (1815-1881) of Baltimore graduated from West Point in 1837, saw duty in the Seminole War and on the Canadian border as an artillery officer. Following the war with Mexico, French was stationed in Texas, but at the outbreak of hostilities in 1861 made his way within the federal lines at Key West. He was commissioned brigadier general and commanded a brigade in Richardson's division, with which he saw action during the Peninsular Campaign, winning  commendation for bravery at Fair Oaks. General French was then raised to command a division in Sumner's Corps, which he led in the magnificent attack that pierced the Confederate center at Sharpsburg and again won commendation. At Fredericksburg, he enthusiastically pressed for the frontal assault on the Confederate positions, claiming that the battle would be won in forty-eight hours. It was doomed to failure, however, and resulted in the slaughter of his division.

French was promoted to major general in November of 1862, was distinguished for meritorious service at Chancellorsville, and commanded elements of the Harpers Ferry garrison during the Gettysburg Campaign. His career with the Army of the Potomac was cut short on the Rappahannock for what General Grant and other ranking officers perceived as failure in the Mine Run operations. After a brief stint as inspector of artillery for the Middle Department, French remained in the army following the end of hostilities, later serving at various stations on the West Coast and at Fort McHenry in Baltimore Harbor.[17]

Rear Admiral **Louis Malesherbes Goldsborough** (1805-1877), born in Washington, D.C., entered the navy at the age of eleven as a midshipman from Maryland. Following service with the Mediterranean fleet and two years at a school in Paris, he was put in command of the newly created Depot of Charts and Instruments in the District of Columbia. In 1837, he resigned from the navy to lead a group of German settlers to Florida and during the

Seminole War took part in the land and sea operations as a volunteer. After his return to the navy, he served in the Mexican War during the bombardment of Vera Cruz and was in command during the attack on Tuxpan. He then participated in an exploring operation in California and Oregon before being appointed superintendent of the United States Naval Academy at Annapolis.

Goldsborough once again served in the Mediterranean and with the Brazilian Squadron before commanding the North Atlantic Squadron at the outbreak of hostilities in 1861. He was instrumental in the planning and implementation of the Burnside expedition to North Carolina that captured Roanoke Island and was promoted to admiral in July of 1862. Rear Admiral Goldsborough was relieved of the difficult task in commanding the far-flung elements in the North Atlantic on September 5, 1862, and was assigned direction of the James River Flotilla. At his own request, he was excused from active duty afloat and assigned the important task of revising naval regulations to better coordinate actions of the expanded wartime navy. Following the war, Goldsborough again saw active duty at sea in command of the European Squadron.[18]

Major General **John Reese Kenly** (1822-1891) of Baltimore practiced law until the outbreak of the war with Mexico, when he raised a company of volunteers in Lieutenant Colonel William H. Watson's battalion. Captain Kenly took part in the capture of Monterey and Victoria, winning commendation for rallying the command in the former engagement on the fall of Watson. Following the expiration of his battalion's term of enlistment, Kenly returned to Baltimore in June 1847, but was soon commissioned major in a regiment raised in Baltimore and Washington. Within a month Major Kenly and his battalion sailed for Vera Cruz and participated in the actions at San Juan and El Paso de Ovejas and carried by assault the works guarding the National Bridge over the Antiqua River. Following the war he resumed his law practice, was twice nominated as a candidate from the Whig party in Maryland, and was commended by the General Assembly of Maryland for distinguished gallantry displayed during the Mexican War.

Following the federal occupation of Maryland, Kenly was commissioned colonel of the First Regiment, Infantry, Maryland Volunteers in June 1861. Relieved from his duty as provost marshal of Baltimore, he accompanied his regiment on guard duty to the upper Potomac and saw action in the Shenandoah Valley. He was subsequently wounded, captured, and paroled during the rout of his regiment by the Maryland Confederates at Front Royal in May 1862. Lincoln promoted him brigadier general in August of that year, and he assumed command of the Maryland Brigade. During General Lee's advance into Maryland that fall, Kenly was given charge of the troops in Baltimore, excepting those in federal forts, and later commanded the defenses at Harpers Ferry. During the Gettysburg Campaign, he served under General William H. French in protecting the Army of the Potomac's supply lines. Upon the reorganization of that army in March of 1864, General Kenly was relieved of field command and given control of a military district in the Middle Department. He held similar positions in the Shenandoah Valley and Maryland's Eastern Shore, and was brevetted major general of volunteers in March of 1865. After the war he resumed his law practice, was active in Union veteran societies, and refused to accept a pension for his war service, saying that he had only done what he felt was his duty.[19]

Major General **Edward Otho Cresap Ord** (1818-1883) of Cumberland graduated from West Point in 1839 and served as an officer of artillery during the Seminole War. He saw duty in various posts along the frontier and was stationed in California during the war with Mexico. Ord was commissioned brigadier general in September 1861 and commanded a division under McDowell in the Shenandoah Valley, in the spring of 1862. Promoted to major general in May of that year, he was transferred to the Army of  the Tennessee. He saw action at Iuka and Corinth, receiving a wound at Hatchie Bridge while leading the pursuit from the latter battle.

General Ord was given command of the XIII Corps following the fall of Vicksburg, and, under orders from Grant, he occupied the Gulf Coast of Texas. Following a leave of absence due to illness, he was assigned to the Army of the James in March of 1864, but, disapproving of Grant's plan of action in the Shenandoah, was relieved of duty at his own request within three weeks. Afterward, he took charge of the Middle Department, which included Baltimore and large parts of Maryland, and was then assigned to command the Department of Virginia and North Carolina in January of 1865. He was recalled to combat duty in March for the final push from the Richmond-Petersburg lines, and was once again wounded, this time at Fort Harrison. He was commended for meritorious service at Dranesville, Iuka, Hatchie, and Fort Harrison and was present when Lee and Grant signed the armistice at Appomattox. Following the war, Ord stayed in the army with the rank of brigadier general and was in charge of various military districts in the West.[20]

Maryland Units in the Confederate Army

The First Maryland Infantry, Confederate States Army, was formed in May of 1861 by combining the Maryland companies formed at Harpers Ferry with those mustered in at Richmond. The regiment was commanded by Colonel Arnold Elzey, Lieutenant Colonel George H. Steuart and Major Bradley T. Johnson.[21]

After a brief campaign in the Valley, the First hastened by train with Joseph E. Johnston's army as it crashed into the flank of Irvin McDowell's Federals at Manassas. Arriving at the critical moment of the battle, the First ignored the warnings of broken and wounded Confederates, and pressed on to where the fire was hottest. Running through the woods and halting at the sight of an unknown line of troops perched on the hill above, Colonel Elzey shouted to his aide-de-camp, Charles Couter of Prince George's county, "Couter, give me a glass—give me a glass quick." At that instant the breeze unfurled the stars and stripes. "Fire!" shouted Elzey, and a crashing volley was delivered. "Charge!" he roared, and all six companies surged up the hill with the war cry. The Yankees did not wait for the confrontation and the First, not stopping to draw breath, bore down on the crumbling Union line. Afterward, General Beauregard galloped up, calling out "Hail! Elzey, Blucher of the day!" The day of the great victory saw Elzey promoted brigadier general, Steuart colonel, Johnson lieutenant colonel, and Captain E.R. Dorsey major.[22] The First then went into camp at Fairfax Station where it was reinforced by recruits from Maryland and reorganized by elections, with many lower ranks passing over higher.[23]

During the campaign of 1862, the First Maryland was in the Shenandoah with Stonewall Jackson as he moved up the Valley. When the First drove in Union pickets before Front Royal on the 23rd of May, a prisoner was asked, "What regiment do you belong to?" "First Maryland," replied the Dutchman.[24] Elated, the regiment stormed through town and came to grips with the Maryland Unionists, commanded by their gallant colonel, John Kenly. Heavy fighting ensued as the Confederates assaulted in front and attempted to turn the flank of the Unionists, who held a position on the crest of some hills supported by artillery and cavalry. Following an artillery duel and movements by cavalry on both sides, Kenly's position became untenable, and he was forced to withdraw. Sensing victory, the Southerners charged, and the rout became general. Almost all of Kenly's command was made prisoner during the pursuit, and its commander was wounded by saber and pistol.[25] For the Unionists, the fight had not been made in vain. Kenly was later commended for buying the army of General Banks valuable time to escape a Jackson trap. It was, however, the sweetest in a long list of victories for the First, CSA, and when word of it reached Maryland there was serious rioting between Union and Confederate sympathizers in Baltimore, Frederick and Hagerstown.[26]

Near the middle of June, Jackson himself was hurrying back down the Valley, trying to avoid being trapped by superior Union forces under generals John C. Frémont and James Shields. The First Maryland was advancing through dense woods in a sharp rear-guard action under generals Ashby and Ewell near Harrisonburg, when it came face-to-face with the Pennsylvania Bucktails. The federals opened fire, dismounting Colonel Johnson and dropping twenty officers and men in the ranks. The colors went down time and again but never touched the ground as the Marylanders stood firm, a rallying point to the shaken Fifty-eighth Virginia. Ewell rushed up. "Charge Colonel!" he ordered. Johnson shouted the unorthodox command, "By the left flank, charge!" and the entire line vaulted forward as one. The Bucktails broke across an open field and in the chase were nearly annihilated. The First Maryland's colors were adorned with a bucktail as a trophy thereafter.[27] The First went on to fight with distinction at Cross Keys, First Cold Harbor, and Malvern Hill.[28]

The Second Maryland Infantry, CSA, was mustered into service at Winchester, on September 28, 1862, and commanded by Major (later Lieutenant Colonel) James R. Herbert of Howard County.[29] It served under General William E. Jones in the Shenandoah Valley performing raiding duty until advancing on Gettysburg with Ewell. En route it was credited with opening the fight that ended in the re-taking of Winchester and the capture of General Milroy's command, with whom served the Union Fifth and Sixth Maryland Infantry and Alexander's Battery. At

Gettysburg the Second participated in the successful assault on Culp's Hill on July 2 and the bloody repulses of the following day. In the ranks arrayed against them stood the First Potomac Home Brigade and the First Eastern Shore Regiment.

Following Gettysburg, the Second was ordered to Hanover Junction, where it was to become part of the Maryland Line then forming under Colonel Bradley T. Johnson. At Cold Harbor, the Second was highly commended for its spontaneous bayonet charge that repulsed elements of Hancock's Corps attempting to breach Lee's works. From that point on it saw continuous action with Ewell's Corps, fighting at White Oak Swamp, Reams' Station, Peeble's Farm, Squirrel Level Road, Hatcher's Run, and Appomattox, where the survivors had the honor of being paroled with Robert E. Lee.[30]

Company B of the Twenty-first Virginia Infantry was mainly composed of members of the Maryland Guard, a famous military organization from Baltimore and one of the finest to enter the Confederate service from the Old Line State. Formed by Captain J. Lyle Clark, the company was kept from joining the First Maryland Regiment, much to its chagrin, to act as a magnet for other Marylanders making their way to Richmond. Following the defeat of General Garnet's Confederates at Phillipi, Clark's company was one of many hastily combined into regiments and sent out under General Robert E. Lee to operate in West Virginia. After serving in the notable campaign against Rosecranz, the Twenty-first, under Colonel William Gilham of the Virginia Military Institute, was assigned to the command of General Stonewall Jackson and took part in the famous Valley Campaign of 1862. Upon expiration of their one year term, Captain Clark's company immediately enlisted in various branches of the Confederate service and fought on faithfully to the final surrender. Known as one of the crack companies in the Army of Northern Virginia, their precision twice caused General Lee to state that it was the best drilled infantry company he ever saw.[31]

The First Maryland Cavalry, CSA, began serving in the Valley in May of 1862, and after continuous recruiting eight companies mustered into service during the following winter. The winter and spring of 1863 found the First with William E. Jones's brigade as it raided western Maryland and the Baltimore & Ohio Railroad, collecting horses and much booty. As Lee thrust into Pennsylvania, the First rode with General Albert G. Jenkins and participated in all the raids and skirmishes of that brigade during the Gettysburg campaign. During the withdrawal, the First checked and counterattacked Union cavalry under Kilpatrick at

Monterey and fought a "desperate hand-to-hand melée in the streets of Hagerstown" in its successful defense of Ewell's supply train and wounded.[32] It served in the Valley again under generals Fitzhugh Lee and Lunsford L. Lomax until autumn when it was ordered to Hanover Junction with the Maryland line.[33]

Outnumbered and outgunned, the First won flowing praise from the Confederacy for saving Richmond from capture during March of 1864. Three thousand Union sabres under Kilpatrick and Dahlgren were harried, from what seemed like all sides, and eventually chased from the outskirts of Richmond by the crafty and tenacious Marylanders.[34] The regiment then fought a delaying action at Beaver Dam Station before moving with Lee and fighting a close and bloody engagement at Pollard's Farm. The regiment then fought with Wade Hampton at Trevilian's Station, where it saved the day by crashing into Custer's flank and routing the federals as they sought to break the Confederate center.

The First then moved north to participate in Jubal Early's advance on Washington and to execute General Lee's adventurous campaign designed to free the fifteen thousand Confederate prisoners at Point Lookout.[35] Under Bradley T. Johnson, the First and Second Maryland cavalry rode through Boonsboro, Sharpsburg and Middletown, invested Frederick, and continued through Westminster, Reisterstown and Cockeysville. Harry Gilmor and the Second burned the same bridges that had been destroyed April 20, 1861, while elements of the First torched Governor Bradford's house in retaliation for the burning of Governor John Letcher's home in Virginia thirty days earlier.[36] With the citizens of southern Maryland alerted and ready to aid the cavalry brigade, Johnson continued his march on Point Lookout by riding across Montgomery and Howard counties to Prince Georges, where he engaged a thousand Union horsemen at Beltsville and drove them pell-mell into Bladensburg.[37] Large Union reinforcements reached Washington and forced Early, fresh from his victory at Monocacy and encumbered as he was with herds of livestock and a wagon train loaded with plunder, to recall Johnson to Silver Spring. Johnson then took up position as the rear guard for the withdrawing Confederate infantry.[38] The First fought holding actions at Rockville and Poolesville, being the last troops to cross safely over the Potomac under the covering fire of the Baltimore Light Artillery.

Shortly after the return to Virginia, the First accompanied General John McCausland on his raid to Chambersburg, Pennsylvania, where, in retaliation for the recent burning of property belonging to prominent Confederates in Shepherdstown and Charlestown, McCausland sent in a written order demanding as indemnity $100,000 in gold and $500,000 in greenback dollars. Although in hiding, the city council proclaimed that the rebels would not dare set fire to Chambersburg, because they were afraid to do so. Within five minutes the town was torched from end to end.[39] After again serving in the Valley with Early, Lomax, and Fitzhugh Lee, the First joined Lee's army before Richmond and rode under William Payne and Thomas "the bravest of the brave" Munford in the withdrawal to Appomattox. Covering Lee's veterans, the First made the last charge of the Army of Northern Virginia, drove back the federals and, refusing to surrender, broke out toward Lynchburg in search of Joe Johnston's Confederates. In his closing address to the Marylanders Munford said:

> Need I say when I see that position so high and almost alone among soldiers, that my heart swells with pride to think that a record so bright and glorious is in some part linked with mine? Would that I could see the mothers and sisters of every member of your [regiment], that I might tell them how nobly you have represented your State and maintained our cause.

> But you will not be forgotten. The fame you have won will be guarded by Virginia with all the pride she feels in her own true sons, and the ties which have linked us together, memory will preserve.

> You who struck the first blow in Baltimore and the last in Virginia have done all that could be asked of you. Had the rest of our officers and men adhered to our cause with the same devotion, today we should have been free from Yankee thralldom. I have ordered the brigade to return to their homes, and it behooves us now to separate.

> With my warmest wishes for your welfare, and a hearty God bless you, I bid you farewell.[40]

Early in 1862, the Second Maryland Cavalry, CSA, was formed by the colorful captain (later colonel) Harry Gilmor of Baltimore County, whose exploits rivaled those of two other famous Confederate horsemen, John Singleton Mosby and Nathan Bedford Forrest. After serving with Stonewall in the Valley campaign, Gilmor and the Second raided profusely throughout Maryland, Virginia, and Pennsylvania, doing great damage and occupying upwards of forty thousand of the enemy in efforts to thwart them. It has been written of his battalion of partisan rangers:

It is but fair to say that a braver, more daring and reckless band never followed the flag of a free companion in the Middle Ages. They were rough and ready; they pervaded the enemy's rear, behind his lines, captured his wagons and couriers carrying dispatches from headquarters to a general in the field, and harassed the enemy without ceasing by day and by night.[41]

In 1864, following Early's campaign in the Valley in which the Second covered itself in glory, the rather independent Gilmor, who once refused promotion to the command of a fine Virginia cavalry regiment in exchange for the release of two of his band from the guardhouse, was promoted to command both the First and Second Maryland Cavalry, and from that point on the records of both units were identical.[42]

Two other mounted units from Maryland served with the Confederacy: Co. K, First Virginia Cavalry, and Co. B, 35th Virginia Battalion (White's) Rangers. Recruited at Leesburg in May of 1861, Co. K was commanded by Captain George R. Gaither and comprised men from Maryland's Eastern Shore. Co. B, formed at Charlottesville in 1862, was commanded by Captain George Chiswell and comprised men from the Poolesville area. Co. B, a wild group, raided its home neighborhood in Montgomery County for horses and armaments and later earned the nickname "Comanches" for its actions in the engagement at Parker's Store. Both units rode with J.E.B. Stuart's feared Black Horse Cavalry in their many exploits including the Seven Day's campaign, Second Manassas, Sharpsburg, Chambersburg, Westminster, Fredericksburg, Brandy Station, Gettysburg, Yellow Tavern, and Appomattox.[43]

In addition to fine infantry and cavalry regiments, Maryland also contributed four crack artillery batteries to the cause of the Confederacy. The First Maryland (Dement's) Artillery, CSA, mustered into service at Richmond in the summer of 1861, by Captain (later Lieutenant Colonel) Richard Snowden, was composed of men from Southern Maryland, the Eastern Shore, and Baltimore City. After serving along the Potomac and on the peninsula, it won laurels for its actions at Seven Pines during the Seven Days' Battles and for its successful and rarely seen charge against deployed infantry at Cedar Run. The First then participated in the Second Manassas campaign, was commended for its actions at Fredericksburg and again at Winchester, then served with Lee at Gettysburg, Mine Run, Cold Harbor, Petersburg, the Weldon Railroad and Sayler's Creek. In all, Captain William F. Dement's command fought in twenty-one engagements before surrendering with the remnants of Lee's army at

Appomattox.44

Organized in the latter part of 1861, the Second Maryland (Baltimore Light) Artillery, CSA, operated along the Rappahannock until fighting with Jackson at Front Royal, Winchester, Bolivar Heights, Fisher's Hill, Harrisonburg and Cross Keys and accompanied him to Richmond for the Seven Days' Battles. Present at Second Manassas and the taking of Harpers Ferry, the Baltimore Light then crossed into Maryland with Lee and the First and Fourth Maryland batteries to win commendations at Sharpsburg. Due to the reorganization of the First Maryland Infantry just after Second Manassas, no regimental-sized units carrying the Maryland state flag accompanied Lee during his first move outside of Virginia. Maryland's three artillery batteries and its fast moving cavalry units presented no magnet for the state's raw recruits who wished to enlist. The presence of the federal army and the short two weeks that Lee spent in Maryland's western counties did not, however, deter young men from answering this heart-felt and interesting proclamation:

> Headquarters Army of N. Va.
> Near Fredericktown, September 8, 1862
>
> To the People of Maryland:
>
> It is right that you should know the purpose that has brought the army under my command within the limits of your State, so far as that purpose concerns yourselves. The people of the Confederate States have long watched with the deepest sympathy the wrongs and outrages that have been inflicted upon the citizens of a commonwealth, allied to the States of the South by the strongest social, political and commercial ties. They have seen with profound indignation their sister State deprived of every right, and reduced to the position of a conquered province. Under the pretense of supporting the Constitution, but in violation of its most valuable provisions, your citizens have been arrested and imprisoned upon no charge and contrary to all forms of law. The faithful and manly protest against this outrage made by the venerable and illustrious Marylander, to whom in better days no citizen appealed for right in vain, was treated with scorn and contempt. The government of your chief city has been suppressed: words have been declared offenses by an arbitrary decree of the Federal

executive, and citizens ordered to be tried by a military commission for what they may dare to speak.

Believing that the people of Maryland possessed a spirit too lofty to submit to such a government, the people of the South have long wished to aid you in throwing off the foreign yoke, to enable you again to enjoy the inalienable rights of freemen and restore independence and sovereignty to your State.

In obedience to this wish, our army has come among you, and is prepared to assist you with the power of its arms, in regaining the rights, of which you have been despoiled.

This, citizens of Maryland, is our mission so far as you are concerned: no restraint on your free will is intended: no intimidation will be allowed. Within the limits of this army at least, Marylanders shall once more enjoy their ancient freedom of thought and speech. We know no enemies among you and will protect all, of every opinion. It is for you to decide your destiny, freely and without constraint. This army will respect your choice, whatever it may be, and while the Southern people will rejoice to welcome you to your natural position among them, they will only welcome you when you come of your own free will.

                    R. E. Lee, General Commanding[45]

After the Sharpsburg campaign, the Baltimore Light went on to fight at Winchester, Gettysburg and the following retreat at Mt. Zion and Hagerstown in Maryland, later at Culpeper Courthouse and Mine Run before joining the Maryland Line. It fought with J.E.B. Stuart at Yellow Tavern, where that great cavalryman died for his cause, rode with Early and Johnson during the Baltimore-Washington campaign of 1864, where it saw action at Catoctin Mountain, Frederick, Poolesville, and raided Chambersburg with McCausland. After being reinforced by Marylanders from Fort Sumter who had enlisted at Baltimore in December of 1860, it became part of Rhett's First South Carolina artillery and the Lucas Battalion of artillery and fought at Maurytown and Woodstock. The Confederacy having no more cannon with which to supply it, the stubborn Second then volunteered for infantry duty in the trenches at Petersburg, and finally surrendered at Appomattox.[46]

Captain Henry Latrobe mustered the Third Maryland (Ritter's) Artillery, CSA, into service at Richmond in January of 1862, where it was sent to Knoxville to campaign with General E. Kirby Smith. One section of the Third fought at Vicksburg, while another, commanded by Sergeant Edward H. Langley, worked the guns of the ram *Queen of the West* as it captured the *Indianola*, a federal ironclad. Yet a third section of Ritter's unit took Union prizes on Deer Creek and saw action at Jackson, Mississippi. Following the fall of Vicksburg, the Third Maryland re-fitted in Alabama and moved on to east Tennessee where it was engaged at Lookout Mountain. It fought in Georgia at Resaca, New Hope Church, Marietta and Atlanta before being ordered back to Nashville. In the last days of the Confederacy, Ritter's guns did service at Mobile and Demopolis before surrendering at Meridian, Mississippi, in May of 1865.[47]

The Fourth Maryland (Chesapeake) Artillery, CSA, was organized early in 1861, but due to a lack of modern cannon was kept in reserve throughout the Peninsula campaign. Finally getting a chance to prove itself, the Fourth, with its outdated smooth-bore weapons, fought so well at Cedar Run[48] that Jubal Early made them a present of four captured Union ten-pounders. The Chesapeake then fought at Warrenton Springs, Bristoe Station, Harpers Ferry, and rolled into Sharpsburg with Lee. After twice seeing action at Hamilton's Crossing near Fredericksburg in 1862 and again in 1863, the battery advanced on Gettysburg with the Army of Northern Virginia and participated in every major engagement with that force until final surrender at Appomattox.[49]

Confederate General and Flag Officers from Maryland

Brigadier General **James J. Archer** (1817-1864), born in Harford County, the fourth son of Doctor John Archer, graduated from the United States Military Academy in 1826. Following frontier duty in the West he resigned and entered the lumber business in Havre de Grace, Maryland, until moving on to San Patricio, Texas, in 1847, where he became a planter. He was commissioned a captain in the Confederate army in March of 1861, and soon after was made colonel and commanded a Texas brigade at the

Evansport batteries. After Seven Pines Archer was promoted brigadier general and led a brigade in A. P. Hill's division, consisting mainly of Tennessee and Alabama regiments. Archer, often noted for his valor, served with distinction under Hill at Mechanicsville, Gaines' Mill, Cedar Mountain, Second Manassas, Harpers Ferry, Sharpsburg, Shepherdstown, Chancellorsville, and Gettysburg, where he was wounded and taken prisoner. General William McComb wrote of Archer:

> In his death, the writer lost one of his warmest friends, Maryland one of her most gallant sons, the brigade the best commander it ever had, and the Confederacy one of the bravest officers in the army—one competent to fill any position in the corps. He could see, decide and act with as much alacrity as any officer I ever knew.

Following a rigorous confinement Archer was exchanged in the summer of 1864, and in spite of pleas from his friends to rest and recover his strength, insisted on immediately returning to active duty. His wounds and the fatigue of another campaign took its toll, and he died in Richmond on the 24th of October, 1864. He lies buried in Hollywood Cemetery, his grave marked by a plain marble shaft.[50]

Brigadier General **Joseph Lancaster Brent** (1826-1905), born in Charles County, attended Georgetown University and moved to California where he practiced law. When war broke out, he sailed for home in the company of William M. Gywnn, ex-United States senator, and Calhoun Benham, United States district attorney in California. The three Confederate sympathizers were arrested on the high seas and held in Fort Lafayette some three weeks before being paroled. Brent, who refused to take an oath  of allegiance, proceeded to Richmond in the winter of 1861-62, and was commissioned captain on the staff of General J. B. Magruder.

Following the Yorktown campaign, Brent was promoted major of artillery and served as chief ordnance officer on the right wing of the Army of Northern Virginia throughout the fighting on the Peninsula in 1862. As a colonel and chief of artillery and ordnance, he was then assigned to western Louisiana under General Richard Taylor where he also commanded the First Louisiana brigade cavalry.

Of the many exploits in which General Brent was engaged, the capture of the Federal ironclad *Indianola* in the spring of 1863 was certainly the most exciting. General Taylor had ordered Brent to take command of two Confederate boats, the *Webb*, a side wheel steamer used as a towboat before the war, and the *Queen of the West*, a federal gunboat captured just days before. He was to engage the powerful ironclad which had run the batteries at Vicksburg and was roaming the Red River. General Brent wasted no time in pursuing the antagonist with his little cotton-bale armored flotilla and went into action twenty miles south of Vicksburg. The 11-inch guns of the formidable *Indianola* could manage but one hit on the *Queen of the West*, doing no damage but scattering a lot of her "defensive armor." Brent's men demoralized the federal gunners with musket volleys every time the *Indianola's* iron shutters were opened to fire the big guns. The *Webb* and *Queen of the West* repeatedly rammed the larger federal boat and forced it to surrender, the Confederates losing but eight men in the engagement.

Brent was promoted brigadier general of cavalry in October of 1864, and held that rank until war's end found him in command of the front line in the West, the last line held by the Confederacy. After being paroled in May of 1865, Brent returned to Baltimore and resumed his law practice before moving to Louisiana in 1870, to engage in planting. He lived in Louisiana until 1888 and twice served in the state legislature before returning once more to Baltimore.[51]

Admiral **Franklin Buchanan** (1800-1874) of Baltimore joined the United States Navy and became a midshipman at the age of fifteen. By 1845, he had attained the rank of commander and was appointed first superintendent of the United States Naval Academy at Annapolis. Buchanan saw action during the Mexican War and accompanied Commodore Mathew Perry during the expedition to open Japan in the 1850s. When the lower South seceded he had been made captain and commanded the Washington naval yard before resigning his commission in April of 1861.

By September Buchanan had entered the Confederate navy as a

captain, and, after overseeing the erection of various shore batteries, he was given command of the ironclad *Virginia (Merrimack)*. Leading this formidable craft during the naval action at Hampton Roads, he sank two of the best federal men-of-war, the *Congress* and *Cumberland*, and three steamers before being wounded. He was promoted to admiral in August of 1862, and assigned to command the defenses and fleet at Mobile Bay. Buchanan again displayed his courage by defending Mobile with the ram C.S.S. *Tennessee* and three small wooden gunboats against federal attack during August of 1864. Eventually, with his gunboats overcome, Buchanan took on Admiral Farragut's entire fleet with his lone ram. When the *Tennessee* would no longer answer her helm and Buchanan himself was again seriously wounded, he finally capitulated. He was exchanged and reassigned to Mobile in March 1865 before surrendering to federal authorities on May 14. Buchanan retired to The Rest, his home on the Miles River in Talbot County, was president of the Maryland Agricultural College in 1868, and thereafter devoted himself to farming.[52]

Major General **Arnold Elzey** (1816-1870) of Somerset County was descended from one of Maryland's oldest families. Elzey dropped his original last name, Jones, for that of his paternal grandmother upon his graduation from West Point in 1837. He served with credit during the Seminole uprising in Florida and in the war with Mexico, being twice brevetted for gallant and meritorious action on the field of battle. Following the fall of Fort Sumter, Elzey, a captain of artillery, surrendered his command of the United States arsenal at Augusta, Georgia, to superior forces and conducted his troops to Washington where he resigned his commission.

After entering the Confederate service, Elzey was by June of 1861 promoted to colonel of the First Maryland Regiment and placed in command of a brigade in General Kirby Smith's division. Before the first battle of Manassas, Elzey addressed his young troops from Maryland:

> In the hour of battle you will remember that you are Marylanders. Every eye from across the waters of the Potomac which separates you from your homes, is upon you, and all those who are dear to us are watching with anxious, beating hearts, the fleshing of your maiden

swords. And they shall not be disappointed, for he had better never been born who proves himself a craven when we grapple with the foeman.

Stirring words, and seemingly not lost on his young troops, with whom he broke and routed the almost victorious army of McDowell. For his gallant actions Elzey was promoted brigadier general and given command of a Virginia brigade, which he led throughout Stonewall Jackson's Valley Campaign and the beginning of the Seven Days' Battle. He was wounded in the leg and had his horse shot out from under him at Port Republic, but bravely pressed on until being seriously wounded at Cold Harbor, a minié ball striking him just above the mouth and passing out behind his left ear.

Following a miraculous recovery, Elzey was promoted major general and in 1863, put in command of the Richmond defenses. In the fall of 1864, he joined General Hood's army of Tennessee as chief of artillery and was active in the operations against Sherman's supply lines. After the war he retired with his wife and son to a small farm in Anne Arundel County. The praise bestowed upon General Elzey is unending: Colonel J.R. Herbert, of Baltimore, called him "a gallant soldier and loved by all who served under him." General Beauregard wrote that he was "brave, zealous and intelligent." Bradley Johnson called him "the soul of chivalry," "a superb soldier," and "the centre and the soul of our [Maryland troops] patriotic day-dreams."53

Commodore **George Nicholas Hollins** (1799-1878) of Baltimore was a midshipman in the navy by the age of fifteen. He saw action in the War of 1812 on the *Erie* as it attempted to break the British blockade of Chesapeake Bay and later on the *President* under Stephen Decatur until captured at Bermuda. In the war with the Barbary pirates, Hollins again served under Decatur with such gallantry that he was awarded a sword in recognition. He attempted to resign his commission as a captain early in 1861, but instead was denied and ordered under arrest by the war department.

Hollins eluded arrest and offered his services to the Confederate States Navy, immediately accepting a commander's commission. He seems to have been the Confederate navy's representative in the "French Lady" incident in June of 1861, capturing the steamer *St. Nicholas* and taking numerous prizes on the Potomac before putting in at Fredericksburg to the accolades of Governor Letcher and Virginia authorities. After a brief stint as head of the shore fortifications on the James River, he was given command of the New Orleans naval station and promptly routed the federal blockading squadron. In December of 1861, Commodore Hollins was then ordered to take a fleet up the Mississippi and assist in the defense of Island No. 10. The arrival of a strong Union fleet at the mouth of the Mississippi brought the commodore hurrying back to New Orleans, but upon arriving he found orders summoning him to Richmond. He had been appointed to the court of inquiry concerning the *Virginia's* destruction, and after absolving her captain of all blame, he and several other older officers were placed on inactive duty. Except for a brief assignment at Columbus, Kentucky, Commodore Hollins remained in that status for the duration of the war and afterwards returned to Baltimore to live out his years.[54]

Brigadier General **Bradley Tyler Johnson** (1829-1903) of Frederick County was the grandson of Colonel Bates Johnson of the Revolutionary Army. He graduated from Princeton in 1849 and from 1851 practiced law in Frederick. He became active in local and state politics, and by 1860 he was chairman of the Democratic Central Committee of Maryland. His Frederick volunteer company of militia was among the first to offer its services in defense of Baltimore and also the first that marched southward to join the Confederacy. Declining a commission as lieutenant colonel in the Virginia service in the hope of organizing a distinctly Maryland command, Johnson was made captain of Company A, First Maryland Regiment. He rose to the rank of major and then lieutenant colonel after fighting at First Manassas and in the Valley Campaign.

In 1862, he was made colonel of the First Regiment and ably commanded his Marylanders at Front Royal, Winchester, Harrisonburg and during the Seven Days' Battles. With his regiment reorganizing after the expiration of their enlistment, Johnson was left without a command as Lee's army maneuvered during the summer of 1862. At the invitation of generals Jackson and Ewell, he was given command of the Virginia brigade of General J.R. Jones, who was temporarily incapacitated. Johnson handled the Virginians magnificently throughout the battle of Second Manassas, his brigade repulsing charge after charge using stones when their ammunition had run out. Afterward Jackson felt compelled to petition the Confederate War Department thus:

> I regarded him as a promising officer when he first entered the army, and so fully did he come up to my expectations that when his regiment was disbanded I put him in command of a brigade, and so ably did he discharge his duties in the recent battles near Bull Run as to make it my duty, as well as my pleasure, to recommend him for a brigadier generalcy. The brilliant service of his brigade in the engagement on Saturday last proved that it was under a superior leader, whose spirit was partaken of by his command.

Following a brief service on the military court in Richmond, Johnson responded to the call of his Marylanders and reached his comrades at Gettysburg on July 2nd. By November he was ordered to Hanover Junction to supervise the organization of the Maryland Line, of which he was elected commander. He was promoted brigadier general of cavalry in June of 1864 for his outstanding exploits in the defense of Richmond and subsequent mounted actions under General Wade Hampton. Johnson accompanied Early in his advance on the federal capital in 1864, and participated in the final campaign in the Shenandoah Valley. During the last few months of the war he was entrusted with the delicate job of maintaining order at a large prisoner-of-war camp in Salisbury, North Carolina. His efforts at restoring order and alleviating prisoner distress in these hectic times were applauded by both sides. Following the war he practiced law in Richmond and twice served in the Senate of Virginia before returning to Baltimore in 1878. General Johnson was immediately enlisted to lead all movements which represented Confederate sentiment in the state, becoming president of the Society of the Army and Navy of the Confederate States in Maryland, and of the Association of the Maryland Line, as well as greatly contributing to the establishment of the Maryland Home for Confederate Veterans.[55]

Brigadier General **Lewis Henry Little** (1817-1862) of Baltimore was the son of a long-time Maryland congressman and a veteran of the War of 1812. The younger Little graduated from West Point in 1839 and later

made captain for gallant conduct at
Monterey during the Mexican War. Little
resigned his commission in May of 1861 and
joined the Confederacy with the rank of
major of artillery, but was soon attached to
General Sterling Price's staff as colonel and
assistant adjutant general. He so
distinguished himself in command of a
brigade at Pea Ridge before Elkhorn Tavern
in the spring of 1862 that he was promoted
to brigadier general upon the
recommendations of Price and General Earl

Van Dorn. After the evacuation of Corinth, Little's division won the
battle of Iuka single-handedly against the forces of Rosecrans, but while
seated on his horse viewing the progress of his fine troops, Little was struck
in the forehead by a minié ball and killed instantly. General Price
expressed the gloom felt by the entire army:

> Than this brave Marylander no one could have fallen
> more dear to me, or whose memory should be more fondly
> cherished by his countrymen. No more skillful officer or
> more devout patriot has drawn his sword in this war of
> independence. He died in the day of his greatest
> usefulness, lamented by his friends, by the brigade of his
> love, by the division he so ably commanded, and by the
> army of the West, of which he had from the beginning
> been one of the chief ornaments.

He was buried by torchlight that September night in Iuka in the garden
behind his headquarters, his remains being later removed to Green Mount
Cemetery in Baltimore.[56]

Major General **Mansfield Lovell** (1822-1884) was born in Washington,
D.C., son of Joseph Lovell, a distinguished Marylander who served as
surgeon general of the United States Army, and grandson of a member of
the Continental Congress. He graduated from West Point in 1842, ninth
in a very famous class, and, as a lieutenant in the Fourth artillery, joined
General Taylor's army in Texas. Following action at Monterey where he
was wounded, Lovell was made aide to General Quitman and participated
in the campaign from Vera Cruz to Mexico City, being again wounded in

the assault at Belasco gate. He was brevetted captain for bravery at Chapultepec, and following the war commanded a battery on the frontier and in New York, where he resigned in 1854. Captain Lovell served as deputy street commissioner, was a member of and drilled the Old City Guard before going South to cast his lot with the Confederacy in 1861.

He was commissioned brigadier general by the Confederate government, but was soon promoted to major general in October of 1861, and given command of Department No. 1, at New Orleans. Due to the small size of his command—there were only arms for 1,200 of his short-term enlisted men—he was compelled to evacuate the city when the federal fleet forced its way past the forts and proceeded upriver. General Lovell withdrew to Vicksburg in December of 1862, where he was superseded by General Van Dorn, and as second in command led the rear guard during the retreat from Corinth. After a court of inquiry relieved Lovell of blame for the surrender of New Orleans, General Joseph E. Johnston recommended that he be given command of a corps in 1864. This was never acted upon, but desiring active duty in the field, Lovell served as a volunteer aide on the staff of General Johnston. General Lovell remained in the South for several years after the war before returning to New York to pursue his civil engineering career.[57]

Brigadier General **William Whann Mackall** (1817-1891) of Cecil County graduated from West Point with General Braxton Bragg in 1837 and served in the Seminole War, where he was severely wounded in 1839. After a brief service along the Canadian border in the early 1840s, Mackall was twice brevetted for gallant and meritorious conduct in the actions at Monterey, Contreras and Churubusco during the Mexican War. He declined the promotion to lieutenant colonel and assistant adjutant general in May of 1861, and joined the Confederate service with the same rank in July. He served as adjutant general on the staff of

General Albert Sidney Johnston until he was promoted brigadier general in February of 1862, and given command of the Confederate forces at Madrid Bend and Island No. 10. He was captured by the federal army under Pope on April 8th and exchanged later that same year.

After leading a brigade in the department of Tennessee and commanding the district of the Gulf, Mackall was appointed chief-of-staff by General Braxton Bragg in April of 1863. Following important services in the campaigns that summer, he was relieved after the battle of Chickamauga at his own request. General Bragg had this to say upon his old classmate's departure:

> With a grateful sense of the distinguished services rendered by this accomplished officer in the high position he has filled, the commanding general tenders him his cordial thanks and wishes him all success and happiness in his future career. The general and the army will long feel the sacrifice made in sparing the services of one so distinguished for capacity, professional acquirements and urbanity.

After commanding the brigades previously under General Hebert in the department of Mississippi and East Louisiana, and serving for a time with General Leonidas Polk, who recommended his promotion to major general, Mackall once again returned to the army of Tennessee and was appointed chief-of-staff under Johnston in January of 1864. He served in the notorious Sherman campaign from Dalton to Atlanta, but declined to continue under Johnston's replacement. He continued to participate in Confederate operations until the capitulation of Lee's army, at which time he surrendered along with generals G.W. Smith and Howell Cobb at Macon, Georgia. After the war, General Mackall returned to Fairfax County, Virginia, where he died in 1891 at Langley, one of his several farms. He is buried at another, Lewinsville, near McLean.[58]

Rear Admiral **Raphael Semmes** (1809-1877) of Charles County was appointed a midshipman in the navy on April 1, 1826, and by the following September saw duty on the *Lexington*, serving with the Mediterranean Squadron for two years. After a leave of absence, during which he studied and practiced law, Semmes rejoined the navy in 1837 and campaigned during the war with Mexico. He commanded the *Sommers* in the blockade of Vera Cruz and was a volunteer aide to Major General Worth in the Tuxpan expedition, being several times commended for gallantry and bravery. From 1847 until resigning his commission in February of 1861,

Commander Semmes worked Prospect Hill, his plantation in Alabama, and performed various duties for the navy. He accepted an appointment as commander in the Confederate States Navy and in April of 1861 was given command of the C.S.S. *Sumter*, a commerce destroyer. After taking many prizes on the high seas Semmes was blockaded at Gibraltar by the United States fleet and forced to lay up his vessel in April of 1862. While planning his return to the Confederacy he was given command of the C.S.S *Alabama*, a formidable cruiser of 1070 tons, soon to be launched for the South from Birkenhead, England. Thus began a record of brilliance and efficiency without equal in the annals of high seas warfare. For twenty-two months the Confederate man-of-war *Alabama* ravaged waters around four continents, ransoming or burning eighty-nine vessels bearing the United States flag. Semmes engaged and sank the U.S.S. *Hatteras* off Galveston, Texas, and in time virtually succeeded in breaking the federal blockade of the South.

By the early summer of 1864, the *Alabama*, unable to put into port for almost two years, needed repairs and the replacement of powder, which had deteriorated in various climates. While lying off the port of Cherbourg, France, awaiting permission from Napoleon III to enter the Imperial Dockyard for overhauling, Captain Semmes espied the U.S.S. *Kearsarge*, which had been pursuing the Confederate raider. In spite of his ship's weakened condition, he sailed out to engage the antagonist. The *Alabama* struck the *Kearsarge* repeatedly and according to naval authorities would have certainly sunk her, but owing to the ineffectiveness of the powder, her shells failed to explode. Following a fierce engagement of over an hour, Semmes realized the hopelessness of his situation and struck the colors. However, the captain of the *Kearsarge* continued to hammer away at the *Alabama*, which eventually went down in a blaze of glory. Captain Semmes and his survivors were picked up by an English yacht and taken to London, where he was received with many honors.

He returned to Richmond in January of 1865, where he was promoted to rear admiral and placed in command of the ironclad squadron on the James River. Upon the fall of the Confederate capital, he burned his ships, formed his men into a land naval brigade and retreated with Lee's army. He was made a brigadier general by President Davis at Danville, Virginia, but the appointment was never made official. Semmes and his sailors were with Major General Joseph E. Johnston a few weeks later when that officer's army surrendered at Durham, North Carolina. He was paroled but then unlawfully arrested and brought to Washington on charges of treason, piracy, mistreating prisoners and violations of the rules of war. He was detained for three months, but eventually all charges were dropped. The government, however, continued to harass Semmes. As a result of this treatment he was unable to hold positions he had procured as a college professor and newspaper editor. Semmes finally returned to Mobile where he set up a law practice. He died and was buried there in 1877. His statue guards the approach to the city from Mobile Bay. Rear Admiral Semmes authored four interesting books, *Service Afloat and Ashore during the Mexican War* (1851), *The Campaign of General Scott in the Valley of Mexico* (1852), *The Cruise of the Alabama and the Sumter* (1864), and *Memoirs of Service Afloat During the War Between the States* (1869).[59]

Brigadier General **George Hume "Maryland" Steuart** (1828-1903) of Baltimore graduated from West Point in 1848 and saw service as an Indian fighter on the western frontier, where he attained the rank of captain of cavalry. Days after the events in Baltimore of April 19, 1861, he resigned and was commissioned captain of cavalry in the regular army of the Confederate States. Steuart was made lieutenant colonel of the First Regiment Maryland Infantry upon its formation and was promoted colonel following the distinguished actions of that unit at the first battle of Manassas. He was promoted to brigadier general in March of 1862, and placed in command of a brigade in Ewell's division, which consisted of four Virginia regiments and the First Maryland. He ably led this unit during Jackson's Valley Campaign until receiving a severe wound in the shoulder at Cross Keys which disabled him for some time. During Lee's invasion of the North in 1863, Steuart commanded a brigade in Johnson's division of Ewell's corps consisting of Virginia and North Carolina regiments as well as the Second Maryland. He commanded this brigade with distinction in the assault on Culp's Hill at Gettysburg and in the Wilderness campaign during which he was captured in the fierce fighting at Bloody Angle. After being taken to Hilton Head by the Federals and being placed under the fire of Confederate batteries, he was exchanged and joined Lee's army at Petersburg. He was assigned command of a brigade in Pickett's division, fought in the center of the battle line at Five Forks and during the Appomattox campaign. After the war General Steuart lived on his farm in Anne Arundel County and served as commander-in-chief of the Maryland division of the United Confederate Veterans. He is buried with many of his comrades in Green Mount Cemetery, Baltimore.[60]

Brigadier General **Allen Thomas** (1830-1907) of Howard County graduated from Princeton in 1850, where he remained to practice law. After marrying the sister of Richard Taylor, later a lieutenant general in the Confederacy, Thomas moved to Louisiana, where he became a planter. At the outset of hostilities in 1861, he organized an infantry battalion and served as major until becoming colonel upon its expansion into the Twenty-ninth Louisiana Infantry in May of 1862. Colonel Thomas served notably at Chickasaw Bluffs during the Vicksburg campaign and was captured when the fortress fell.

Following his parole he was assigned to collect and organize paroled prisoners west of the Mississippi, attaining the rank of brigadier general on February 4, 1864. He was given charge of five Louisiana regiments and a battalion in General Taylor's department and later was promoted to divisional command. Being rather young when the war ended, General Thomas went on to have a diverse and noteworthy career. He was a planter, presidential elector, professor and member of the board of supervisors at Louisiana State University, coiner of the New Orleans branch mint, and U.S. consul and minister to Venezuela. He was nominated for Congress in 1876, but declined.

Brigadier General **Lloyd Tilghman** (1816-1863) of Talbot County was the great-grandson of Matthew Tilghman, who had been president of the revolutionary conventions of Maryland, member of the legislature and

Continental Congress and known as the Patriarch of Maryland. Lloyd graduated from West Point in 1836 and was commissioned second lieutenant in the First Dragoons. He resigned that same year to pursue construction engineering and was employed with a number of railroads in the South until the outbreak of the Mexican War. He served as a volunteer aide to General David Twiggs in the battles of Palo Alto and Resaca de la Palma, and was later captain of the Maryland and District of Columbia Battalion of volunteers. Following a return to the railroad profession, Tilghman joined the army of the Confederate States in 1861 and was commissioned brigadier general.

Early in 1862 he was given the important job of inspecting forts Donelson and Henry on the Tennessee River and was placed in direct command of the latter. Due to defects in the location of Fort Henry, Tilghman knew that his 2,600 men and eleven guns would be no match for General Grant's 12,000-plus men and his seven gun-boats in early February of 1862. He therefore transferred his cavalry, infantry, and field artillery to Fort Donelson and resolved to make a stubborn fight with a small force and his siege guns. Disdaining to abandon his heroic defenders, General Tilghman remained and himself worked one of the guns, refusing to surrender for hours, even after the enemy had breached the walls. He and his gallant band of one hundred men had permitted the remainder of the garrison to reach Fort Donelson in safety, tore great holes in the advancing Federals, and disabled a gun-boat—all at the loss of five men killed and sixteen wounded.

Following his exchange in August of 1862, he rejoined the Army of the West and was put in command of the First brigade in Loring's division. General Tilghman led a spirited rearguard action after the battle of Corinth, Mississippi, in May of 1863. He dismounted to direct the fire of his artillery at the battle of Baker's Creek (Champion's Hill) when he was struck by a shell fragment that tore through his body. He was interred at Vicksburg, and now lies in Woodlawn Cemetery, New York City.[61]

Major General **Isaac Ridgeway Trimble** (1802-1888) of Culpeper County, Virginia, graduated from West Point in 1822, and served as engineer and lieutenant of artillery. In 1832, he resigned and became chief

engineer of the Baltimore and Susquehanna railroad and a succession of other Eastern and Southern lines. During this period he identified himself almost completely with the state of Maryland and accepted command of the volunteer un-uniformed corps of Baltimore after the events of April 1861. He engaged in the burning of the bridges north of Baltimore, but following the federal move through Annapolis and the subsequent occupation of Maryland, Trimble entered the service of Virginia in May of 1861, as lieutenant colonel of engineers.

He was first assigned by General Lee to construct the defenses at Norfolk, then in August commissioned brigadier general to command a brigade in Ewell's division. Trimble was conspicuous for gallantry and leadership during the Valley Campaign of 1862, especially at Cross Keys, where in command of two brigades, he held off superior numbers, and when reinforced, counterattacked and put Frémont's Federals to flight. His brigade further distinguished itself during the Seven Days' Battles, with Trimble personally leading a successful charge against federal defenses at Cold Harbor. He again fought with gallantry against Pope at Slaughter's Mountain, and with five hundred exhausted troops seized strategic Manassas Junction in the enemy's rear, capturing men, guns, and the immense federal provisions. Jackson congratulated him on his great success and recommended him for promotion to major general, later writing in his official report: "I regard the capture of Manassas Junction Station at night, after a march of thirty-four miles without food, as the most brilliant achievement that has come under my notice during the war."

General Trimble was severely wounded at Second Manassas and promoted major general in January of 1863. Upon his return he was honored by being assigned command of Jackson's old division, but because of a lingering ailment associated with his wound he was unfit for duty in the field. Lee gave him time to recuperate by assigning him command of the valley of Virginia, with orders to form into brigades "under you all the Maryland troops—a measure I have much at heart." His health was much improved by mid-summer of 1863, but with no suitable command available General Trimble offered his services as voluntary aide to Ewell during the Gettysburg campaign. When General Pender fell on the first day of the great battle, Trimble was given command of his division in A.P.

Hill's corps. He led two brigades of this division in Pickett's assault on the federal center and was so severely wounded that he was captured and subsequently lost a leg.

Despite earnest efforts to procure his earlier release, General Trimble, despised in the North as the "bridge burner" of Baltimore, was imprisoned at Johnson's Island and Fort Warren and finally exchanged in February of 1865, for two federal major generals. He hastened to rejoin General Lee, but before doing so the army had surrendered. His bravery, chivalry, and capacity for leadership won for him the highest rank and greatest fame of all Maryland's soldiers in the War Between the States. After the war he made his home in Baltimore and is buried in Green Mount Cemetery.[62]

Brigadier General **Robert Charles Tyler** (1833-1865) of Baltimore moved to Memphis in 1860, where he enlisted as a private in Company D, Fifteenth Tennessee Infantry in April of 1861. He soon won promotion to regimental quartermaster and in the fall was commissioned major on the staff of Cheatham. He continued his meteoric rise by being promoted to lieutenant colonel of the Fifteenth Tennessee, which he led at the battles of Belmont and Shiloh. Following  convalescence from a wound and the reorganization of his regiment at Corinth, Tyler was promoted to colonel and served as provost marshal during the invasion of Kentucky in the latter half of 1862. He saw distinguished service in the Army of Tennessee, but was seriously wounded at Missionary Ridge in November of 1863, resulting in the loss of a leg and a long recuperation. Tyler was promoted brigadier general in February of 1864, and while resting near West Point, Georgia, he organized other wounded Confederates and elements of the state militia to repulse a Union cavalry raid under Wilson. It was at West Point, Georgia, April 1865, in an earthwork called Fort Tyler, that the general led a group of 265 resolute men against overwhelming odds. With General Tyler on crutches and with but a few pieces of artillery, the garrison refused to surrender and defended their bastion until completely overrun. A sharpshooter's bullet ended the career of the gallant Tyler, who lies buried at the little earthen fort that bore his name.[63]

 Brigadier General **Charles Sidney Winder** (1829-1862) of Talbot County also comes from an old and prestigious Maryland family. His line boasts two Maryland governors (his grandfathers) and relations the likes of John Eager Howard and Francis Scott Key. He was graduated from West Point in 1850 and was promoted captain for heroism in 1855. His reward for actions during a hurricane aboard a troop ship in the Atlantic made him the youngest man in the army to hold that rank. Following service against the Indians in Washington Territory, where he again excelled, Winder resigned his commission on April 1, 1861, and was appointed a major of artillery in the Confederate Army. After taking part in the bombardment of Fort Sumter, he was commissioned colonel of the Sixth South Carolina Infantry in July of 1861. Winder then hurried northward, but ended up just missing the action at First Manassas.

Colonel Winder was promoted to brigadier general in March of 1862 and given command of the Stonewall Brigade in General Jackson's division. He led this famous brigade of five Virginia regiments throughout the Valley Campaign of 1862, playing a conspicuous part in the advance during the battle of Port Republic, and accompanied Jackson to Richmond for the Seven Days' Battles. General Winder led his brigade and five others, including the First Maryland, in the furious assault at Gaines' Mill that broke the federal center. Of this famous action Jackson reported, "Thus formed, they moved forward under the lead of that gallant officer, whose conduct here was marked by the coolness and courage which distinguished him on the battle-fields of the valley." It was during the subsequent advance against Pope that Winder, in command of Jackson's old division (Stonewall having been elevated to corps command), received a mortal wound while directing his batteries in the artillery duel at Cedar Mountain. Although ill, he left his ambulance and rode to the head of his column on August 9, 1862, where he was struck by a shell and died within a few hours. In the official reports Lee paid tribute to Winder's "courage, capacity, and conspicuous merit," while Jackson wrote:

> It is difficult within the proper reserve of an official report
> to do justice to the merits of this accomplished officer.
> Richly endowed with those qualities of mind and person
> which fit an officer for command, and which attract the

admiration and excite the enthusiasm of troops, he was rapidly rising to the front rank of his profession, and his loss has been severely felt.

General Winder lies buried at Wye House, near Easton in Talbot County, Maryland.[64]

Brigadier General **John Henry Winder** (1800-1865) of Somerset County graduated from West Point and later was an instructor of tactics there when Jefferson Davis was a cadet. He resigned from the army in 1823 but was re-commissioned in 1827 and saw service in the Seminole and Mexican wars, being brevetted major and lieutenant colonel for gallant and meritorious conduct during the latter conflict. He resigned his commission as major in April of 1861 and was appointed brigadier general in the provisional Confederate Army. Following his appointment as commander of the Department of Henrico, Winder was made provost marshal of Richmond, a difficult job that called upon him to maintain order in the overcrowded capital, put him in charge of the arrest and return of deserters and later made him responsible for the prison camps in the vicinity.

After serving as department commander to the Second District of North Carolina and Southern Virginia with headquarters at Goldsboro, General Winder was put in charge of Andersonville prison in June of 1864, and was made commissary general for all prisoners east of the Mississippi the following November. He performed his duties admirably, though was criticized by his own people and those in the North for his actions in what amounted to a thankless and impossible job. The Northern press accused him of deliberately starving Union prisoners, a charge that is utterly without foundation. The federal government's refusal to exchange prisoners of war, a tactic aimed at the Confederacy's limited manpower resources in relation to the Union, handicapped Winder in the performance of his duties. He made every effort to provide the prisoners with the same ration received by the Confederate soldiers in the field, meager as that was because of the Union blockade. Finally, broken down by his unenviable task, Winder died at Florence, South Carolina, in February of 1865 and now lies in Green Mount Cemetery in Baltimore.[65]

Notes

Introduction

1. Charles Lewis Wagandt, *The Mighty Revolution: Negro Emancipation in Maryland, 1862-1864* (Baltimore: The Johns Hopkins University Press, 1964), 11.
2. George L. Radcliffe, *Governor Thomas H. Hicks of Maryland And The Civil War* (Baltimore: Lord Baltimore Press, 1901), 54-55.

Chapter One: Maryland Before The War

1. Clement A. Evans, ed., *Confederate Military History* (Atlanta, Ga: Confederate Publishing Co., 1899), vol. 2, *Maryland and West Virginia*, by Bradley T. Johnson, 6. Hereafter cited as Johnson, *Maryland.*
2. Richard Walsh, and William Fox, eds., *Maryland, A History 1632-1974* (Baltimore: Maryland Historical Society, 1974), 2.
3. Ibid., 2.
4. Johnson, *Maryland*, 7.
5. Ibid.
6. Ibid., 8.
7. Walsh, *Maryland, A History*, 109-110.
8. Johnson, *Maryland*, 10.
9. Clement, A. Evans, ed., *Confederate Military History* (Atlanta, Ga: Confederate Publishing Co., 1899), vol. 1, *The South as a Factor in the Territorial Expansion of the United States*, by William R. Garrett, 59-246. Hereafter cited as Garrett, *Expansion.*
10. James M. McPherson, *Ordeal by Fire, The Civil War and Reconstruction* (New York: Alfred A. Knopf, 1982), 2.
11. Ibid.
12. John C. Calhoun, *A Discourse on the Constitution and Government of the United States* (New York: D. Appleton and Company, 1856), 306-308, 338-340.
13. McPherson, *Ordeal by Fire*, 42.
14. F. Bancroft, *Calhoun and the South Carolina Nullification Movement* (Gloucester, Mass.: P. Smith, 1966), 109-116.
15. Ibid., 163-186.
16. Harold R. Manakee, *Maryland in the Civil War* (Baltimore: Maryland Historical Society, 1961), 18.
17. Jean H. Baker, *The Politics of Continuity, Maryland Political Parties from 1858 to 1870* (Baltimore: The Johns Hopkins University Press, 1973), 10-11.
18. Manakee, *Maryland in the Civil War*, 20.

19. Baker, *The Politics of Continuity*, xiv.
20. Ibid., 19.
21. Ibid., 19.
22. Ibid., 15-17.
23. Ibid.
24. Calhoun, *A Discourse on the Constitution*, 356-358, 379-381, 390-391.
25. William J. Evitts, *A Matter of Allegiances, Maryland from 1850 to 1861* (Baltimore: The Johns Hopkins University Press, 1974), 24, 54.
26. Manakee, *Maryland in the Civil War*, 18.
27. Baker, *The Politics of Continuity*, 6-16.
28. J. Thomas Scharf, *History of Maryland from the Earliest Period to the Present Day*, 3 vols. (Annapolis: General Assembly of Maryland, 1879; repr., Hatboro, Pennsylvannia: Tradition Press, 1967), 361-64; Mathew Page Andrews, *History of Maryland: Province and State* (Doubleday, Doran & Co., 1929; repr., Hatboro, Pennsylvannia: Tradition Press, 1965), 511.
29. McPherson, *Ordeal by Fire*, 265-279.
30. Manakee, *Maryland in the Civil War*, 14.
31. W. Darrell Overdyke, *The Know-Nothing Party in the South* (Baton Rouge: Louisiana State University Press, 1950), 103-105, 265-266; Laurence F. Schmeckebier, *History of the Know Nothing Party in Maryland* (Baltimore: The Johns Hopkins University Press, 1899).
32. Evitts, *A Matter of Allegiances*, 2.
33. Ibid., 3.
34. Baker, *The Politics of Continuity*, 5.
35. *Baltimore Sun*, August 26, 1859.
36. *Cecil Democrat (Elkton)*, June 5, 1858.
37. Baker, *The Politics of Continuity*, 25.
38. Ibid.
39. Penelope Campbell, *Maryland in Africa: The Maryland State Colonization Society, 1831-1857* (Columbus: Ohio State University Press, 1971); *Baltimore Sun*, November 6, 1858.
40. Baker, *The Politics of Continuity*, 25.
41. Oswald G. Villard, *John Brown, 1800-1859, A Biography Fifty Years After* (New York: Alfred A. Knopf, 1943), 312-315; Evitts, *A Matter of Allegiances*, 124.
42. *Cecil Democrat (Elkton)*, October 22, 1859.
43. Manakee, *Maryland in the Civil War*, 5.
44. Wagandt, *The Mighty Revolution*, 8.
45. *Baltimore Sun*, October 21 and 25, 1859.
46. Ibid., October 21, 1859.
47. Ibid., October 20, 1859.
48. *Herald and Torch Light (Hagerstown)*, November 1, 1859.
49. Johnson, *Maryland*, 11.
50. *Baltimore Sun*, November 7, 1859.
51. *Frederick Herald*, November 8, 1859.
52. *Planter's Advocate (Upper Marlboro)*, October 26, 1859; Baker, *The Politics of Continuity*, 26.
53. *Frederick Examiner*, March 14, 1860.
54. Baker, *The Politics of Continuity*, 28.
55. James M. Wright, *The Free Negroes of Maryland, 1634-1860*, Columbia University Studies in History, Economics and Public Law, vol. 97 (New York: Columbia

University Press, 1921), 315.

56. Baker, *The Politics of Continuity*, 28.

57. *Frederick Examiner*, December 14, 1859.

58. *Baltimore Sun*, March 5, 1860.

59. Baker, *The Politics of Continuity*, 39.

60. Evitts, *A Matter of Allegiances*, 145.

61. Ollinger Crenshaw, *The Slave States in the Presidential Election of 1860* (Gloucester, Mass.: Peter Smith, 1969), 112-113.

62. *Montgomery County Sentinel*, June 20, 1860.

63. *Baltimore Sun*, September 7, 1860.

64. John P. Kennedy, "Journal", May 9, August 2, 1860, *Kennedy Papers*, Peabody Library, Baltimore.

65. Crenshaw, *The Slave States in Election of 1860*, 113.

66. Evitts, *A Matter of Allegiances*, 146.

67. Ibid., 113.

68. *Baltimore American*, Nov. 2, 1860

69. *Baltimore Daily Clipper*, Nov. 5, 1860.

70. *Baltimore American*, April 27, 1860.

71. Crenshaw, *Slave States in Election of 1860*, 119.

72. Ibid.

73. Ibid.

74. Ibid.

75. Speech at Iddin's Store, October 13, 1860, *Blair Papers*.

76. Crenshaw, *Slave States in the Election of 1860*, 121.

77. *Annapolis Gazette*, November 1, 1860.

78. Baker, *The Politics of Continuity*, 38.

79. *Der Deutsche Correspondent (Baltimore)*, April 15, December 15, December 22, 1860.

80. *Port Tobacco Times*, October 11, 18, 1860; *Baltimore Daily Exchange*, November 5, 1860.

81. J. H. Parks, *John Bell of Tennessee* (Baton Rouge: Louisiana State University Press, 1950).

82. Evitts, *A Matter of Allegiances*, 137.

83. Ibid., 138.

84. *Daily Baltimore Republican*, February 10, 1860.

85. *Eastern Star*, February 21, 1860.

86. Crenshaw, *Slave States in the Election of 1860*, 118.

87. *Baltimore Sun*, November 6-15, 1860.

88. Ibid., November 8, 1860.

Chapter Two: The Secession Winter

1. David M. Potter, *The Impending Crisis 1848-1861* (New York: Harper and Row, 1976), 424.

2. Clement A. Evans, ed., *Confederate Military History* (Atlanta, Ga.: Confederate Publishing Co., 1899), vol. 1, *The Civil History of the Confederate States*, by Clement A. Evans. Hereafter cited as Evans, *Civil History*.

3. Potter, *The Impending Crisis*, 439-40, 454-5, 464, 477-8, 485, 489-90, 501, 552.

4. *Baltimore Sun*, November 7, 1860.

5. Ibid., November 8, 21, 22, 1860.

6. Radcliffe, *Governor Hicks and the Civil War*, 19.

7. Ibid., 23.

8. See James H. Brewer, *The Confederate Negro, Virginia's Craftsmen and Military Laborers 1861-1865* (Durham, NC: Duke University Press, 1969).

9. Evans, *Civil History*, 317-318.

10. James Buchanan, *Mr. Buchanan's Administration on the Eve of the Rebellion* (New York: D. Appleton and Co., 1866), 115-116.

11. Ibid., 119-120.

12. *New York Herald*, December 5, 1860; *New York Tribune*, December 7, 1860.

13. Radcliffe, *Governor Hicks and the Civil War*, 41-42.

14. Buchanan, *Mr. Buchanan's Administration*, 134-153.

15. Ibid., 136.

16. Evitts, *A Matter of Allegiances*, 159.

17. Buchanan, *Mr. Buchanan's Administration*, 139-144.

18. Ibid., 140.

19. Ibid., 142.

20. Baker, *The Politics of Continuity*, 47.

21. *Baltimore Sun*, December 19, 20, 1860; *Baltimore Daily Clipper*, March 18, 28, 1861.

22. *Baltimore Sun*, January 4, 1861.

23. Evitts, *A Matter of Allegiances*, 166.

24. *Baltimore Sun*, January 11 and 12, 1861.

25. Evitts, *A Matter of Allegiances*, 164.

26. Buchanan, *Mr. Buchanan's Administration*, 144-152.

27. Bradley, *Maryland*, 13.

28. Ibid.

29. *Baltimore Sun*, February 18, 20, 1861.

30. National Archives, Broadside, "To the People of Frederick County," *Civil War Papers*, Record Group 59, records of the Department of State.

31. William Glenn, "Civil War Diary of William Glenn," January 1861, *Glenn Papers*, Maryland Historical Society.

32. *Baltimore American*, February 20, 1861.

33. Confederate States of America, President, *A Compilation of the Messages and Papers of the Confederacy, Including the Diplomatic Correspondence 1861-1865* (Nashville: James D. Richardson, United States Publishing Co., 1905), 33.

34. Manakee, *Maryland in the Civil War*, 24.

35. Ibid., 28.

36. Ibid.

37. Potter, *The Impending Crisis*, 562; *Baltimore Sun*, February 25, 1861.

38. Norma Cuthbert, ed., *Lincoln and the Baltimore Plot, 1861* (San Marino: Huntington Library, 1949), 133-135.

39. Ward Hill Lamon, *Recollections of Abraham Lincoln 1847-1865* (Chicago: A.C. McClurg and Co., 1895), 261.

40. *Baltimore Sun*, February 25, 1861.

41. Maryland, *Documents of the Senate of 1858*, Document "B."

42. Evitts, *A Matter of Allegiances*, 161.

43. Ibid.

44. Radcliffe, *Governor Hicks and the Civil War*, 17.

45. *Baltimore Sun*, January 19, February 3, 1861.

46. Ibid., January 10, 1861.

47. Ibid., January 15, 1861.

48. *Baltimore American*, January 7, 1861.

49. Radcliffe, *Governor Hicks and the Civil War*, 44.

50. Ibid., 45.

51. Ibid., 46.

52. Ibid., 41.

53. *Baltimore American*, February 4, 1861.

54. Ibid., February 2, 1861.

55. Manakee, *Maryland in the Civil War*, 29.

56. Maryland, *Letter Book of the Executive*, Hall of Records, Annapolis.

57. Radcliffe, *Governor Hicks and the Civil War*, 50.

58. Johnson, *Maryland*, 16.

59. Ibid., 17.

60. Confederate President, *Papers of the Confederacy*, 84.

61. Ibid., 89.

62. Ibid., 91.

63. Ibid., 74.

64. *New York Tribune*, July 7, 1862.

65. Ibid., November 9, 1860.

Chapter Three: The South's First Casualty

1. Manakee, *Maryland in the Civil War*, 30-31.

2. Johnson, *Maryland*, 17.

3. George William Brown, *Baltimore and the Nineteenth of April, 1861* (Baltimore: N. Murray, 1887), 12.

4. Johnson, *Maryland*, 19.

5. Manakee, *Maryland in the Civil War*, 31; Evitts, *A Matter of Allegiances*, 177.

6. Ibid., 178.

7. Ibid., 179; Johnson, *Maryland*, 20.

8. Radcliffe, *Governor Hicks and the Civil War*, 54.

9. Johnson, *Maryland*, 20.

10. Ibid., 21.

11. Manakee, *Maryland in the Civil War*, 34.

12. Johnson, *Maryland*, 21.

13. Brown, *Baltimore and the Nineteenth of April*, 46-55.

14. Manakee, *Maryland in the Civil War*, 35.

15. Johnson, *Maryland*, 21.

16. Brown, *Baltimore and the Nineteenth of April*, 46-55.

17. Evitts, *A Matter of Allegiances*, 180.

18. *Baltimore Sun*, April 22, 1861.

19. *Lincoln Papers*, April 18, 1861, Library of Congress, Washington, D.C.

20. Manakee, *Maryland in the Civil War*, 37.

21. Radcliffe, *Governor Hicks and the Civil War*, 54-55.

22. Ibid., 55.

23. Brown, *Baltimore and the Nineteenth of April*, 56.

24. Ibid., 58.

25. Manakee, *Maryland in the Civil War*, 38.

26. *Boston Courier*, April 19, 1861.

27. Manakee, *Maryland in the Civil War*, 38.

28. *New York Herald*, April 20, 1861; *New York Daily Tribune*, April 23, 1861.

29. Radcliffe, *Governor Hicks and the Civil War*, 56.
30. Maryland, *Journal of the Senate of 1861*, 64.
31. Maryland, *House Documents of 1861*, Document G; Radcliffe, *Governor Hicks and the Civil War*, 56-57.
32. Brown, *Baltimore and the Nineteenth of April*, 70.
33. Manakee, *Maryland in the Civil War*, 39.
34. Johnson, *Maryland*, 23.
35. Manakee, *Maryland in the Civil War*, 153.
36. Ibid., 40.
37. Ibid., 42; Johnson, *Maryland*, 23-24.
38. Brown, *Baltimore and the Nineteenth of April*, 60, 75.
39. Johnson, *Maryland*, 24.
40. Radcliffe, *Governor Hicks and the Civil War*, 58-59.
41. Evitts, *A Matter of Allegiances*, 182.
42. *Baltimore Sun*, April 23, 24, 1861.
43. Radcliffe, *Governor Hicks and the Civil War*, 60.
44. *Baltimore Sun*, April 30, 1861.
45. Radcliffe, *Governor Hicks and the Civil War*, 60.
46. Manakee, *Maryland in the Civil War*, 49.
47. Johnson, *Maryland*, 29.
48. Manakee, *Maryland in the Civil War*, 44.
49. Henry S. Humphreys, *Songs of the Confederacy* (Willis Music Company: Cincinnati, 1961), 26.
50. In the third stanza the references are to Charles Carroll of Carrollton, one of the four Maryland signers of the Declaration of Independence, and to Lt. Col. John Eager Howard, famous Revolutionary officer from Maryland. Those in the fourth stanza are to Major Samuel Ringgold and Colonel William H. Watson, Maryland heroes of the Mexican War, and to Governor Enoch Lowe and Congressman Henry May, both Marylanders who strongly defended states rights.
51. Johnson, *Maryland*, 46.
52. Ibid., 46.
53. Maryland, *House Documents 1861-62*, Document A.
54. Radcliffe, *Governor Hicks and the Civil War*, 63.
55. *Baltimore Sun*, April 25, 1861.
56. Maryland, *House Documents, 1861-62*, Document A.
57. Radcliffe, *Governor Hicks and the Civil War*, 70.
58. Maryland, *House Documents, 1861-62*, Document A.
59. Maryland, *Journal of the Senate*, April 27, 1861.
60. Maryland, *Journal of the House of Delegates*, April 27, May 8, 1861.
61. Ibid., April 29, 1861.
62. Ibid., May 1, 3, 1861.
63. Johnson, *Maryland*, 29.
64. Manakee, *Maryland in the Civil War*, 50.
65. Johnson, *Maryland*, 30.
66. Maryland, *Journal of the House of Delegates*, 106; *House Documents of 1861*, Doc. F.
67. Radcliffe, *Governor Hicks and the Civil War*, 89.
68. Johnson, *Maryland*, 27-28.
69. "A Virginia Girl's Address to her Lover" (1861), State Department Records, cited in Baker, *The Politics of Continuity*, 54.
70. James A. Marshall, ed., *Private and Official Correspondence of General Benjamin F.*

Butler (Norwood, Mass.: Plimpton Press, 1917), Butler to General Scott, May 8, 1861.

71. William McHenry Howard, *Recollections of a Maryland Confederate Soldier and Staff Officer under Johnston, Jackson and Lee* (Baltimore: Williams and Wilkins Co., 1914), 28-73.

72. Johnson, *Maryland*, 42-43.

73. Ibid., 42-43.

74. Radcliffe, *Governor Hicks and the Civil War*, 95.

75. Ibid., 96.

76. Ibid., 95.

77. Samuel Tyler, *Memoir of Roger Brooke Taney* (Baltimore: John Murphy and Co., 1872), 427.

78. Walker Lewis, *Without Fear of Favor: A Biography of Chief Justice Roger Brooke Taney* (Boston: Houghton Mifflin, 1965).

79. McPherson, *Ordeal By Fire, 152*.

80. Maryland, *Letter Book of the Executive*.

81. Radcliffe, *Governor Hicks and the Civil War*, 98.

82. Ibid.

83. Maryland, *Journal of the Senate*, 143.

84. Ibid., 152.

85. Ibid., 251-54.

86. Maryland, *Journal of the House of Delegates*, 170.

87. *War of the Rebellion: A Compilation of the Official Records of the Union and Confederate Armies*, 128 vols. (Washington, D.C.: Government Printing Office, 1880-1901), 2: 673. Hereafter cited as *Official Records*.

88. Maryland, *Letter Book of the Executive*.

89. Maryland, *House Documents of 1861*, Document H.

90. Maryland, *Senate Documents of 1861*, Documents J & K.

91. *Official Records*, series i, 2: 138-156.

92. Maryland, *Senate Documents of 1861*, Document M.

93. Daniel Carroll Toomey, *The Civil War in Maryland* (Baltimore: Toomey Press, 1983), 29.

94. Manakee, *Maryland in the Civil War*, 56.

95. Ibid., 47-61.

96. Johnson, *Maryland*, 35.

97. Ibid.

98. Baker, *The Politics of Continuity*, 54-55.

99. Johnson, *Maryland*, 44.

100. Ibid., 39.

101. Ibid., 39-40.

102. *Official Records*, series i, 5: 614.

103. Henry Kyd Douglas, *I Rode With Stonewall* (New York: 1940).

104. Edwin W. Beitzell, *Point Lookout Prison Camp for Confederates* (St. Mary's City, MD: St. Mary's County Historical Society, 1967), 115-176.

105. Manakee, *Maryland in the Civil War*, 55.

106. Compare the Declaration of Independence by the state of South Carolina of 1860 to the Declaration of Independence of the American Colonies of 1776.

107. Evitts, *A Matter of Allegiances*, 183.

108. Johnson, *Maryland*, 17.

Chapter Four: The Trampled Ballot

1. *Official Records*, series ii, 1: 609.
2. Johnson, *Maryland*, 94.
3. Ibid., 95.
4. Manakee, *Maryland in the Civil War*, 56.
5. Wagandt, *The Mighty Revolution*, vii.
6. Johnson, *Maryland*, 95.
7. Radcliffe, *Governor Hicks and the Civil War*, 120-121.
8. Ibid., 119-121.
9. Thomas E. Griess, ed., *The West Point Military History Series: Atlas for the American Civil War* (Wayne, NJ: Avery Publishing Group, 1986), 33.
10. Baker, *The Politics of Continuity, Maryland Political Parties from 1858 to 1870* (Baltimore: The Johns Hopkins University Press, 1973), 87; Only 52,000 votes were counted in 1863.
11. Marshall, *(Official Correspondence of General Benjamin F. Butler)*, 1: 26-27.
12. Walsh, *Maryland, A History*, 362-364.
13. Baker, *The Politics of Continuity*, 106.
14. Wagandt, *The Mighty Revolution*, 253-254.
15. See United States, President (1861-1865: Lincoln), *A Proclamation by the President of the United States of America* (Washington, D.C.: War Department, Adjutant General's Office, 1863).
16. Ibid.
17. *The Debates of the Constitutional Convention of the State of Maryland, Assembled at the City of Annapolis, Wednesday, April 27, 1864* (Annapolis: Richard P. Bayley, 1864), 3: 1325-1458.
18. Scharf, *History of Maryland*, 570-74.
19. Walsh, *Maryland, A History*, 368-69.
20. *Baltimore American*, January 5, 1864.
21. E.B. Long, *The Civil War Day by Day, An Almanac 1861-1865* (New York: Da Capo Press, 1985), 583.
22. *Baltimore Sun*, January 24, 1862.
23. *Baltimore American*, February 27, 1862; Walsh, *Maryland, A History*, 365.
24. Baker, *The Politics of Continuity*, 79-80.
25. Ibid., 84.
26. Ibid., 85-86.
27. Augustus Bradford, from James Touchstone, September 29, 1863, *Bradford Papers*, Maryland Historical Society, Baltimore.
28. Ibid., Bradford to Hicks, December 29, 1862.
29. *Baltimore Clipper*, April 23, 1863.
30. Henry Winter Davis, *Speeches and Addresses* (New York: Harper Brothers, 1867), 265-291.
31. Baker, *The Politics of Continuity*, 97.
32. *Cecil Whig (Elkton)*, March 14, 1863.
33. Manakee, *Maryland in the Civil War*, 57-59.
34. United States Congress, *Report on Military Interference at Elections* 38th Congress, 1st session., 1864, Senate Executive Document 14, Serial No. 1176, pp. 4-5.
35. Baker, *The Politics of Continuity*, 90.
36. *Baltimore American*, November 3, 1863.
37. Ibid.

38. *Baltimore Sun*, November 4, 1863.
39. Baker, *The Politics of Continuity*, 89.
40. *Baltimore Sun*, November 5-10, 1863.
41. Ibid., April 2, 1864.
42. Blair to Thomas Swann, *Blair Papers*, October 17, 1863, Library of Congress, Washington, D.C.
43. *Baltimore Sun*, April 6-12, 1864.
44. *Debates of the Constitutional Convention*, 2:1037-53.
45. Ibid., 2:1052, 1067.
46. Ibid., 1:664, 681.
47. Ibid., 2: 787-90, 800, 820-30.
48. Ibid., 2: 830-31; *Proceedings of the State Convention of Maryland to Frame a New Constitution* (Annapolis, 1864), 265-66, 273-77.
49. McPherson, *Ordeal by Fire*, 393.
50. Josiah Henry Benton, *Voting in the Field* (Boston: Private Printing, 1915), 223-249.
51. *Baltimore Sun*, November 9-15, 1864.
52. *Maryland Union (Frederick)*, March 3, 1862.
53. Manakee, *Maryland in the Civil War*, 60.
54. *Baltimore American*, April 1, 1864.
55. Baker, *The Politics of Continuity*, 134-135.
56. *Maryland Journal (Towson)*, August 5, 1865.
57. *Bel Air Aegis and Intelligencer*, August 4, 1865.
58. Thomas Swann, to the General Assembly, *Swann Executive Papers*, Privately Owned, as cited in Baker, *The Politics of Continuity*, 143.
59. Maryland, *House and Senate Documents, Extra Session, 1866*, Document A.
60. *Baltimore Daily Gazette*, April 16, 1866.
61. *Frederick Republican Citizen*, June 22, 1866.
62. *Baltimore American*, May 9, 1866.
63. Ibid., June 15, 1866.
64. Ibid., June 22, 1866.
65. *Baltimore Sun*, October 20, 1886.
66. Ibid., November 7-13, 1866.
67. Maryland, *House and Senate Documents, 1867*, Document A.
68. *Baltimore Daily Gazette*, February 16, 1867.
69. William S. Myers, *The Self-Reconstruction of Maryland, 1864-1867* (Baltimore: J.H. Press, 1909), 43-45.
70. *Debates of the Constitutional Convention*, 1: 664, 681.
71. *Baltimore Sun*, September 19-24, 1867.
72. *St. Mary's Beacon (Leonardtown)*, September 5, 1867.
73. *Baltimore American*, March 6, 1868.
74. Baker, *The Politics of Continuity*, 187.
75. *Cumberland Alleganian*, November 6, 1868.
76. *Baltimore Sun*, March 17, 1866, October 17, 1867.

Chapter Five: Maryland's Place In History

1. Harry Wright Newman, *Maryland and the Confederacy* (Annapolis, MD: Private Printing, 1976), 48.
2. Radcliffe, *Governor Hicks and The Civil War*, 115.
3. Howard, *Recollections*, 406.

Chapter Six: Marylanders in Battle

1. Isaac R. Trimble, "Marylanders in the Confederate Army," *Southern Historical Society Papers* (Richmond), 37: 235.

2. Johnson, *Maryland*, 98.

3. Ibid., 155.

4. Jackson's Brigadiers, June 8, 1862, Steuart, Elzy, Trimble, and later Winder. Howard, *Recollections, 122-125.*

5. Manakee, *Maryland in the Civil War*, 108-133.

6. Ibid., 57-58.

7. Radcliffe, *Governor Hicks and the Civil War, 120.*

8. Douglas Southall Freeman, *Lee's Lieutenants, A Study in Command* (New York: Charles Scribner's Sons, 1942), 377-82.

9. Charles Camper, and J.W. Kirkley, *Historical Record of the First Regiment Maryland Infantry* (Washington: Gibson Brothers, 1871); Manakee, *Maryland in the Civil War*, 109-110.

10. The General Assembly of Maryland, *History and Roster of Maryland Volunteers, War of 1861-5* (Baltimore: Press of Guggenheimer, Weil & Co., 1898); Manakee, *Maryland in the Civil War*, 110-119.

11. Johnson, *Maryland*, 98.

12. General Assembly, *Maryland Volunteers of 1861-5*, 460-646; Manakee, *Maryland in the Civil War*, 119-124.

13. General Assembly, *Maryland Volunteers of 1861-5*, 701-44.

14. Frederick William Wild, *Memoirs and History of Captain F.W. Alexander's Baltimore Battery of Light Artillery, U.S.V.* (Baltimore: Press of the Maryland School for Boys, 1912).

15. *Biographical Cyclopedia of Representative Men of Maryland and D.C.* (Baltimore, 1879), 696-97; Manakee, *Maryland in the Civil War*, 143.

16. Robert Underwood Johnson, and Clarence Cough Buel, eds., *Battles and Leaders of the Civil War* (New York: Century Co., 1887), 2: 333, 3: 587, 590-91, 595, 4: 350-57, 506-20; Manakee, *Maryland in the Civil War*, 143.

17. Johnson, *Battles and Leaders of the Civil War*, vols. 2-4; Manakee, *Maryland in the Civil War*, 143-144.

18. *Official Records*, vol. ii, ix; vol. iv, xiii; vol. xi, xxiii; vol. xvii, xxx; Johnson, *Battles and Leaders of the Civil War*, 1: 640, 666, 2: 151, 169, 264, 4: 634.

19. *Biographical Cyclopedia of Representative Men of Maryland and D.C.*, 588-89; Manakee, *Maryland in the Civil War*, 145-46; Camper and Kirkley, *Historical Record of the First Regiment, Maryland Infantry.*

20. *Battles and Leaders of the Civil War*, 2: 311-12, 731-34, 753, 3: 531-35, 598, 4: 107, 346, 487, 579, 709, 716-34; Manakee, *Maryland in the Civil War*, 146.

21. W.W. Goldsborough, *The Maryland Line in the Confederate Army, 1861-65* (Baltimore: Guggenheimer, Weil & Co., 1900), 11.

22. Howard, *Recollections, 34-43.*

23. Ibid., 46-62.

24. Johnson, *Maryland*, 71.

25. Ibid., 70-73.

26. Manakee, *Maryland in the Civil War*, 57.

27. Johnson, *Maryland*, 77-80.

28. Goldsborough, *The Maryland Line*, 9-81.

29. Ibid., 88.

30. Ibid., 90-159.

31. Ibid., 160-62.

32. Johnson, *Maryland*, 113.

33. Goldsborough, *The Maryland Line*, 165-236.

34. Johnson, *Maryland*, 117-118.

35. Jubal A. Early, *War Memoirs, Autobiographical Sketch and Narrative of the War Between the States* (Bloomington: Indiana University Press, 1960), 385-86.

36. Harry Gilmor, *Four Years in the Saddle* (New York: Harper and Brothers, 1866), 191-203; Robert E. Mitchell, *Colonel Harry Gilmor's Raid Around Baltimore* (Baltimore: Erbe Publishers, 1976), 4-26.

37. Johnson, *Maryland*, 123-129.

38. Brad Coker, *The Battle of Monacacy* (Baltimore: University of Baltimore Honors Monograph Series, 1982), 46-48.

39. Johnson, *Maryland*, 129-130.

40. Ibid., 132-133.

41. Goldsborough, *The Maryland Line*, 241-148???

42. Ibid., 244; Gilmor, *Four Years in the Saddle*, 230, 184-291.

43. Goldsborough, *The Maryland Line*, 249-56; Manakee, *Maryland in the Civil War*, 137-138.

44. Tunstall Smith, *Richard Snowden Andrews, Lieutenant-Colonel, Commanding the First Maryland Artillery, (Andrews Battalion), Confederate States Army, A Memoir* (Baltimore: Press of the Sun Job Printing Office, 1910).

45. Johnson, *Maryland*, 89-90; Douglas Southall Freeman, *Lee's Lieutenants* (New York: Charles Scribner's Sons, 1943), 2: 156-57.

46. Goldsborough, *The Maryland Line*, 275-95; Johnson, *Maryland*, 101-33, 142.

47. Manakee, *Maryland in the Civil War*, 140-141.

48. Early, *War Memoirs*, 96-97.

49. Goldsborough, *The Maryland Line*, 319-28.

50. *Biographical Cyclopedia*, 43-44; Daniel D. Hartzler, *Marylanders in the Confederacy* (Silver Spring, Maryland: Family Line Publishers, 1986), 3-4.

51. Hartzler, *Marylanders in the Confederacy*, 6; Johnson, *Maryland*, 182-84.

52. Hartzler, *Marylanders in the Confederacy*, 4-5; Manakee, *Maryland in the Civil War*, 148-49; Johnson, *Maryland*, 155-56.

53. Esmeralda Boyle, *Biographical Sketches of Distinguished Marylanders* (Baltimore: Kelly, Piet & Co., 1877), 309-318.

54. William Harwar Parker, Capt., *The Confederate States Navy* (London: Thomas Yoseloff, 1962), 15-16, 55-60; Johnson, *Maryland*, 156-57; Hartzler, *Marylanders in the Confederacy*, 6.

55. *Biographical Cyclopedia*, 655-56; Goldsborough, *The Maryland Line*, 122-24; Johnson, *Maryland*, 174-182.

56. Ezra J. Warner, *Generals in Gray, Lives of the Confederate Commanders* (Baton Rouge: Louisiana State University Press, 1959), 188-89; Johnson, *Maryland*, 169-70.

57. Johnson, *Maryland*, 162-63; Hartzler, *Marylanders in the Civil War*, 8.

58. Warner, *Generals in Gray*, 203-04; Johnson, *Maryland*, 172-74; Hartzler, *Marylanders in the Confederacy*, 8-9.

59. Harry Wright Newman, *The Maryland Semmes and Kindred Families* (Baltimore: Maryland Historical Society, 1956), 76-80.

60. Warner, *Generals in Gray*, 290-91; Johnson, *Maryland*, 167-69; Manakee, *Maryland in the Civil War*, 152.

61. Warner, *Generals in Gray*, 306; Johnson, *Maryland*, 163-65; Hartzler, *Marylanders*

in the Confederacy, 11.

62. Freeman, *Lee's Lieutenants*; Warner, *Generals in Gray,* 310-11; Johnson, *Maryland,* 159-62.

63. Hartzler, *Marylanders in the Confederacy,* 12.

64. *Official Records,* 12: pt. 2, 178, 183; Howard, *Recollections,* 101, 119, 162-169, etc.; Johnson, *Maryland,* 165-77.

65. Warner, *Generals in Gray,* 340-41; Manakee, *Maryland in the Civil War,* 153-54.

BIBLIOGRAPHY

Primary Sources

Blair, Montgomery. *The Montgomery Blair Papers*. Library of Congress, Washington, D.C..

Bradford, Augustus. *Bradford Papers*. Maryland Historical Society, Baltimore.

Civil War Papers. Broadside, "To the People of Frederick County." Record Group 59, Records of the Department of State, National Archives, Washington, D.C..

Confederate States of America, President. *A Compilation of the Messages and Papers Of The Confederacy, Including the Diplomatic Correspondence 1861-1865*. Nashville: United States Publishing Co., James D. Richardson, 1905.

Davis, Henry Winter. *Speeches and Addresses*. New York: Harper Brothers, 1867.

Glenn, William. "Civil War Diary of William Glenn." The Glenn Papers, Maryland Historical Society.

Kennedy, John P. "Journal." The John P. Kennedy Papers, Peabody Library, Baltimore.

Lamont, Daniel S., Secretary of War. *The War of the Rebellion: A Compilation of the Official Records of the Union and Confederate Armies*. Washington, D.C.: Government Printing Office, 1897.

Lincoln, Abraham. "The Robert Todd Lincoln Collection of Abraham Lincoln Papers." Library of Congress, Washington, D.C.

Marshall, James A., ed., *Private and Official Correspondence of General Benjamin F. Butler*. Norwood, Mass.: Plimpton Press, 1917.

Maryland. *The Debates of the Constitutional Convention of the State of Maryland, Assembled at the City of Annapolis, Wednesday, April 27, 1864*. Annapolis: Richard P. Bayly, 1864.

_____. *Documents of the Senate of 1858*. Hall of Records, Annapolis, MD.

_____. *History and Roster of Maryland Volunteers, War of 1861-65*. Baltimore: Press of Guggenheimer, Weil & Co., 1898.

_____. *House Documents of 1861, 1862*. Hall of Records, Annapolis, MD.

_____. *House and Senate Documents, 1867.* Hall of Records, Annapolis, MD.

_____. *House and Senate Documents, Extra Session, 1866.* Hall of Records, Annapolis, MD.

_____. *Journal of the House of Delegates.* Hall of Records, Annapolis, MD.

_____. *Journal of the Senate.* Hall of Records, Annapolis, MD.

_____. *Letter Book of the Executive.* Hall of Records, Annapolis, MD.

_____. *Proceedings of the State Convention of Maryland to Frame a New Constitution.* Annapolis, MD: 1864.

Moore, Frank. *The Rebellion Record, A Diary of American Events, with Documents, Narratives, Illustrative Incidents, Poetry, Etc..* New York: G. P. Putnam, 1862.

Nicolay, John G. and John Hay. *Abraham Lincoln, Complete Works, Comprising His Speeches, Letters, State Papers, and Miscellaneous Writings.* New York: The Century Co., 1907.

United States, Congress. *Report on Military Interference at Elections.* 38th Congress., 1st Session., 1864.

United States, President, (1861-1865: Lincoln). *A Proclamation by the President of the United States of America.* Washington, D.C.: War Department, Adjutant General's Office, 1863.

Newspapers

Annapolis Gazette. 1 November 1860.

Baltimore American. 27 April 1860; 2 November 1860; 7 January; 4, 20 February 1861; 27 February 1862; 5 January; 1 April 1864; 9 May; 15, 22 June 1866; 6 March 1868.

Baltimore Daily Clipper. 5 November 1860; 18, 28 March 1861; 23 April 1863.

Baltimore Daily Exchange. 5 November 1860.

Baltimore Daily Gazette. 16 April 1866.

Baltimore Sun. 6, 7 November 1858; 26 August; 20, 21, 25 October 1859; 5 March; 7, September; 7, 8, 21, 22 November; 19, 20 December; 1860; 4, 10, 11, 12, 15, 19 January; 3, 18, 20 February; 22-24, 30 April 1861; 24 January 1862; 4-10 November 1863; 2, 6-12 April; 9-15 November 1864; 17 March; 20 October; 7-13 November 1866; 19-24 September; 17 October 1867.

Bel Air Aegis and Intelligencer. 4 August 1865.

Cecil Democrat (Elkton). 5 June 1858; 22 October 1859.

Cecil Whig (Elkton). 14 March 1863.

Cumberland Alleganian. 6 November 1868.

Daily Baltimore Republican. 10 February 1860.

Der Deutsche Correspondent (Baltimore). 15 April; 15, 22 December 1860.

Easton Star. 21 February 1860.

Frederick Examiner. 14 December 1859; 14 March 1860.
Frederick Herald. 8 November 1859.
Frederick Republican Citizen. 22 June 1866.
Herald and Torch Light (Hagerstown). 1 November 1859.
Maryland Journal (Towson). 5 August 1865.
Maryland Union (Frederick). 3 March 1862.
Montgomery County Sentinel. 20 June 1860.
New York Herald. 5 December 1860; 20 April 1861.
New York Daily Tribune. 9 November; 7, December 1860; 23 April 1861.
Planter's Advocate (Upper Marlboro). 26 October 1859.
Port Tobacco Times. 11, 18 October 1860.
St. Mary's Beacon (Leonardtown). 5 September 1867.

Secondary Works

Andrews, Mathew Page. *History of Maryland: Province And State.* Baltimore: Doubleday, Doran & Co., Inc., 1929.

Baker, Jean H. *The Politics of Continuity, Maryland Political Parties from 1858 to 1870.* Baltimore: The Johns Hopkins University Press, 1973.

Bancroft, F. *Calhoun and the South Carolina Nullification Movement.* Gloucester, Mass., P. Smith, 1966.

Beitzell, Edwin W. *Point Lookout Prison Camp for Confederates.* Baltimore: Maryland Historical Society, 1967.

Benton, Josiah Henry. *Voting In The Field, A Forgotten Chapter of the Civil War.* Boston: Privately Printed, 1915.

Biographical Cyclopedia of Representative Men of Maryland and D.C. Baltimore: 1879.

Booth, George Wilson. *Personal Reminiscences of a Maryland Soldier in the War Between the States, 1861-1865.* Baltimore: Press of Fleet, McGinley & Co., 1898.

Boyle, Esmeralda. *Biographical Sketches of Distinguished Marylanders.* Baltimore: Kelly, Piet & Co., 1877.

Brewer, James H. *The Confederate Negro, Virginia's Craftsmen and Military Laborers 1861-1865.* Durham, NC: Duke University Press, 1969.

Brown, George William. *Baltimore and the Nineteenth of April, 1861.* Baltimore: N. Murray, 1887.

Buchanan, James. *Mr. Buchanan's Administration on the Eve of the Rebellion.* New York: D. Appleton & Co., 1866.

Calhoun, John C. *A Disquisition on Government and a Discourse on the Constitution and Government of the United States.* New York: D. Appleton & Co., 1863.

Campbell, Penelope. *Maryland in Africa, The Maryland State Colonization Society 1831-1857.* London: University of Illinois Press, 1971.

Camper, Charles and J.W. Kirkley. *Historical Record of the First Regiment Maryland Infantry*. Washington, D.C.: Gibson Bros., 1871.

Coker, Brad. *The Battle of Monocacy*. Baltimore: University of Baltimore Honors Monograph Series, 1982.

Crenshaw, Ollinger. *The Slave States in the Presidential Election of 1860*. Baltimore: The Johns Hopkins University Press, 1945.

Cuthbert, Norma, ed., *Lincoln and the Baltimore Plot, 1861*. San Marino, CA: Huntington Library, 1949.

Davidson, Laura Lee. *The Services of the Women of Maryland to the Confederate States*. Baltimore: A Prize Essay, Baltimore Chapter of the Daughters of the Confederacy, 1920.

Douglas, Henry Kyd. *I Rode With Stonewall*. New York: Privately Printed, 1940.

Early, Jubal Anderson. *War Memoirs, Autobiographical Sketch and Narrative of the War Between the States*. Lynchburg, VA: R.H. Early, 1912.

Evans, Clement A., ed., *Confederate Military History*. Atlanta, Ga.: Confederate Publishing Co., 1899. 12 vols. and a supplement, vol. 13.

_____. *The Civil History of the Confederate States*. see *Confederate Military History*. vol, 1.

Evitts, William J. *A Matter of Allegiances, Maryland from 1850 to 1861*. Baltimore: Johns Hopkins University Press, 1974.

Freeman, Douglas Southall. *Lee's Lieutenants, A Study in Command*. New York: Charles Scribner's Sons, 1943.

Garrett, William R. *The South as a Factor in the Territorial Expansion of the United States*. See Evans, Clement A., ed., *Confederate Military History*, vol. 1.

Gilmor, Harry, Colonel. *Four Years in the Saddle*. New York: Harper & Brothers, Publishers, 1866.

Goldsborough, W. W. *The Maryland Line in the Confederate Army 1861-1865*. Baltimore: Guggenheimer, Weil & Co., 1900.

Greiss, Thomas E., ed. *Atlas for the American Civil War*. The West Point Military History Series. Wayne, NJ: Avery Publishing Group Inc., 1986.

Harrison, Mrs. Burton. *Recollections Grave and Gray*. New York: Charles Scribner's Sons, 1911.

Hartzler, Daniel D. *Marylanders in the Confederacy*. Silver Spring, MD: Family Line Publishers, 1986.

Howard, McHenry. *Recollections of a Maryland Confederate Soldier and Staff Officer under Johnston, Jackson and Lee*. Baltimore: Williams & Wilkins Co., 1914.

Humphreys, Henry S. *Songs of the Confederacy*. Cincinnatti: Willis Music Co., 1961.

Huntsberry, Thomas V. and Joanne M. Huntsberry. *Maryland in the Civil War*. Private Printing, 1985.

Johnson, Bradley T. *Maryland and West Virginia*. see Evans, Clement A., ed., *Confederate Military History*. vol. 2.

Johnson, Robert Underwood and Clarence Clough Buel. *Battles and Leaders of the Civil War*. New York: The Century Co., 1887.

Klein, Frederic Shriver. *Just South of Gettysburg, Carroll County, Maryland in the Civil War*. Westminster, MD: Newman Press, 1963.

Lamon, Ward Hill. *Recollections of Abraham Lincoln 1847-1865*. Chicago: A.C. McClurg & Co., 1895.

Lewis, Walker. *Without Fear of Favor: A Biography of Chief Justice Roger Brooke Taney*. Boston: Houghton Mifflin, 1965.

Long, E.B. *The Civil War Day by Day, An Almanac 1861-1865*. New York: Da Capo Press, 1985.

Manakee, Harold R. *Maryland in the Civil War*. Baltimore: Maryland Historical Society, 1961.

Marks, Bayly Ellen and Mark Norton Schatz. *Between North and South, A Maryland Journalist Views the Civil War, The Narrative of William Wilkins Glenn 1861-1869*. London: Associated University Presses, 1976.

McPherson, James M. *Ordeal by Fire, The Civil War and Reconstruction*. New York: Alfred A. Knopf, 1982.

Michel, Robert E. *Colonel Harry Gilmor's Raid Around Baltimore July 10th to 13th, 1864*. Baltimore: Erbe Publishers, 1976.

Myers, William S. *The Self-Reconstruction of Maryland, 1864-1867*. Baltimore: The Johns Hopkins University Press, 1909.

Newman, Harry Wright. *The Maryland Semmes and Kindred Families*. Baltimore: Maryland Historical Society, 1956.

Overdyke, W. Darrell. *The Know-Nothing Party in the South*. Baton Rouge: Louisiana State Univeristy Press.

Parker, William Harwar, Capt. *The Confederate States Navy*. London: Thomas Yoseloff, 1962.

Parks, J. H. *John Bell of Tennessee*. Baton Rouge: Louisiana State University Press, 1950.

Potter, David M. *The Impending Crisis 1848-1861*. New York: Harper & Row, Publishers, 1976.

Radcliffe, George L. *Governor Thomas H. Hicks of Maryland and the Civil War*. Baltimore: Lord Baltimore Press, 1901.

Redcay, W. Harold and G. Thomas LeGore. *Just South of Gettysburg, Carroll County, Maryland in the Civil War, Personal Accounts and Descriptions of a Maryland Border County, 1861-1865*. Westminster, MD: The Newman Press, 1963.

Scharf, J. Thomas. *History of Maryland from the Earliest Period to the Present Day*. Annapolis: General Assembly of Maryland, 1879.

_____. *History of the Confederate States Navy from Its Organization to the Surrender of Its Last Vessel*. New York: Rogers & Sherwood, 1887.

Schmeckebier, Laurence F. *History of the Know-Nothing Party in Maryland*. Baltimore: The Johns Hopkins University Press, 1899.

Smith, Tunstall. *Richard Snowden Andrews, Lieutenant-Colonel, Commanding the First Maryland Artillery, (Andrews Battalion), Confederate States Army, A Memoir*. Baltimore: Press of the Sun Job Printing Office, 1910.

Toomey, Daniel Carroll. *The Civil War in Maryland*. Baltimore: Toomey Press, 1983.

Trimble, Isaac R. "Marylanders in the Confederate Army." *Southern Historical Society Papers*. vol. 37.

Tyler, Samuel. *Memoir of Roger Brooke Taney*. Baltimore: John Murphy & Co., 1872.

Vandiver, Frank E. *Jubal's Raid, General Early's Famous Attack on Washington in 1864*. London: McGraw-Hill, 1960.

Villard, Oswald G. *John Brown, 1800-1859, A Biography Fifty Years After*. New York: Alfred A. Knopf, 1943.

Wagandt, Charles Lewis. *The Mighty Revolution: Negro Emancipation in Maryland, 1862-1864*. Baltimore: The Johns Hopkins University Press, 1964.

Walsh, Richard and William Lloyd Fox. *Maryland, A History 1632-1974*. Baltimore: Maryland Historical Society, 1974.

Warner, Ezra J. *Generals in Gray, Lives of the Confederate Commanders*. Baton Rouge, LA: Louisiana State University Press, 1959.

Wild, Frederick William. *Memoirs and History of Capt. F.W. Alexander's Baltimore Battery of Light Artillery, U.S.V.*. Baltimore: Press of the Maryland School for Boys, 1912.

Wright, James M. *The Free Negroes in Maryland, 1634-1860*. New York: Columbia Univeristy Press, 1921.

Index